HEALING AT THE WELL

HEALING AT THE WELL

Mike Endicott

Terra Nova Publications

First published in Great Britain in 2000. This revised edition 2012
Published in USA by CreateSpace by arrangement with the UK publisher

Published in Great Britain by
Terra Nova Publications International Ltd,
PO Box 2400, Bradford-on-Avon, Wiltshire BA15 2YN, England

ISBN 978-1469935874

Contents

Preface

Mike Endicott's ministry has been an immense blessing to the family of God in south-east Wales and it is a joy to see how it is being extended beyond our neighbourhood in all sorts of ways.

Mike has emerged as one of the outstanding teachers in the Church here and any reader of this book will at once see why. He is entirely honest about his feelings and struggles; entirely realistic, and often very funny, in his assessment of our dim, human capacities; entirely focused on the goodness of God, so that we are reminded all the time of the dangers of treating God like a heavenly mail-order catalogue, trying to reduce God to our scale of priorities.

What you will read here is both a moving personal story about what disablement can mean for a deeply anointed Christian ministry, and a whole series of profound reflections on the nature of our God and of His healing work.

Everything flows from how we learn the patience to stand under the Cross of Jesus, because when we are there we see what he sees, the infinite glory and love of the Father. That is where the healing fountains start.

I thank God for Mike and what he has taught me and so many others and I pray that God will bless this marvellous testimony.

Archbishop Rowan Williams

Foreword

There is nothing more impressive than a changed life! And it was through a totally changed life that I first met Mike.

"You're different," I said to a friend a few years ago. "What's happened to you?"

"I met a blind man in Wales," she replied, and then mystified me further by adding, "I've been going every week to see him at the Well." The mental picture of a man with a white stick sitting by a village pump was obviously not what she wanted to convey. I had never seen her eyes looking bright and 'alive' before; she had been crippled by emotional pain ever since we met.

"This man, Mike Endicott, he's been praying for me," she explained. "God works through him so powerfully. He's helped me face things in my past which have been destroying all my relationships ever since." I could certainly see she was different. It is always a mystery, why some people stay emotionally disabled by life's traumas while others grow even stronger through them. I wanted to know more about this blind man and his remarkable ministry.

My next encounter with Mike was through a tape my friend lent me. I listened to it on the M25 and was so fascinated I forgot the traffic jam completely! Mike had been talking at a conference, and I guess what he said contained the seeds of this book. He shared the pain he had felt as blindness gradually encroached on his active life; his struggle with understanding why a loving God could allow this to happen to him; and then how he had begun to realise God wanted to transform his pain into healing grace for others. Suddenly, I realised the 'Well' was indeed a wayside water supply, but of the spiritual kind! Mike told us on the tape how he, and a group of friends, had prayed their vision into reality; and out of a derelict chapel in South

Wales they had created a healing centre where many could come, drink and be refreshed.

There was something compelling about the voice on the tape. An unusual combination of power and gentleness; humility and boldness; calm acceptance and pig-headed determination.

It was not difficult for my friend to persuade me to go with her to the Well! Since God healed me so remarkably after eight years in a wheelchair, I have visited some magnificent healing centres all round the country. Beauty and comfort combine to prepare us to receive God's touch but, to me, the Well still looked like a dilapidated old chapel from the outside. Inside, it was hardly luxurious, but the moment I crossed the threshold I knew Jesus was there.

It was a training day, and the large room was filled with people who had once come to the Well broken, hopeless and wounded by life, but they had met Jesus, been changed by him, and now they wanted to learn how they too could be used by him as instruments of peace and healing.

A tall, handsome man came striding towards me through the crowd, beside a beautiful black guide dog and I knew I had, at last, met the Reverend Michael Endicott in person.

Since then, I have heard him speak at many conferences, watched him ministering to streams of people long into the night, and been greatly helped and blessed through attending various of his 'schools of ministry' —but he still remains one of the most humble men I know.

Mike not only believes Jesus can mend broken hearts and broken bodies, he also believes Jesus can use the broken to rescue the broken. His desire to teach and empower ordinary lay people to become the hands of Jesus is one of the most exciting parts of Mike's vision.

I do not want to spoil the book for you by telling you too much. As you read it, you will meet Mike yourself, visit the Well and the people who work there. This is not just a personal story of suffering overcome, nor is it an account of the birth of a new Christian organisation—it is very much more than that. I believe it will be of deep interest to anyone who is grappling with suffering and all the question marks that surround it. I strongly recommend that you read it, because I know you will enjoy it enormously. I believe this book will help us all to capture just a tiny part of this blind man's vision of Jesus himself.

Jennifer Rees Larcombe

Introduction

One day, a donkey fell down a well. Perhaps he was not looking where he was going and just fell into the hole in the ground. The farmer who owned the hapless animal, assuming it to be dead, decided to bury it where it lay rather than go to all the trouble of hauling the dead weight up and out of the well. He began to bury it by shovelling barrow loads of earth down into the well shaft on top of the donkey. But the animal was far from being dead. Each time he was covered, the donkey struggled up through the layer of earth, snorted with exasperation and stood waiting for the next barrow load. Each time, it came and covered him. Each time, he struggled upwards, snorting and shaking off the soil. Peering down into the gloom, the farmer could still see the uncovered donkey's back and continued to work. The harder he worked the higher became the pile of earth underneath the donkey. He struggled and snorted ever upwards until eventually, to the farmer's great joy and surprise, he came to the top of the well and climbed out into the fresh air.

This is the story of another kind of donkey: a young life, full of vigour and promise, which became disastrously buried by the incurable onslaught of blindness. This is an account of how that disability, contrary to all society's normal expectation, has been conquered and turned around to work for God through the ministry of healing and wholeness in the Christian Church. This story is not so much a chronology of events leading to the present day, but a working through of the age-old question, 'How can there be a good God in the face of all the suffering to be found in the world?'

There may be no definite answers to questions such as this, but, through searching for some of those answers, there is peace in adversity, life in death and victory in defeat.

But let all who take refuge in you be glad;
let them ever sing for joy.
Spread your protection over them,
that those who love your name may rejoice in you.

Psalm 5:11 [NIV]

1

HAPPY DAYS

A clergy friend from South Wales looked at me over his cup of coffee and dog collar, in the kitchen at the Well Centre, and giggled out loud.

"You must admit, Mike," he chortled, "there's something very amusing about all this. How can a blind man stand up in front of a group of people and offer to pray for their healing?" Geoff giggled a bit more, adding, "Come to think of it, how does a blind man get to run a Christian healing centre, anyway?"

"Only God really knows," I replied, "but there must be a message in there, somewhere!"

Over the following few days, I began to question whether or not I should try to set down on paper the events which had led up to the position in which I now find myself, knowing that those events are wrapped up to the greatest extent with a developing relationship with God rather than anything else.

Here I am, the leader of a multi-denominational community of prayerful people to whom God has entrusted the gift of ministering to others, yet one would naturally expect that I need to be on the receiving end of His grace, as much as anyone! The following extract from a local magazine serves to highlight the paradox:

THE WELL CENTRE is run by a registered charity called the Cwmbran Mission of Christian Healing and takes its spiritual authority through its chaplain, to the Bishop of Monmouth.

The Centre is not a church, but a place where people come to receive the benefits of the Church's Ministry of Healing and Wholeness from a team of highly trained people who minister in quiet love and acceptance.

Most of the work is run on an appointment system and is private and confidential, offering times of listening, prayer and ministry to those needing God's help in their lives. Those who come are ordinary Christian folk from all walks of life, both lay people and leaders, and the Centre's catchment area is roughly from North Wales to Plymouth, from Portsmouth to Nottingham, Derby, Sheffield and Birmingham, although some come from further afield.

The range of problems encountered is broad; it includes ill health of all kinds, but extends to poor relationships with others and with God, all sorts of past hurts and present difficulties and to those who simply wish to see their relationship with God grow deeper.

Teaching days at the Well encourage others to grow as Christians, to minister themselves, and such teaching often extends by request into churches right across the catchment area.

Far from being an Advice Bureau, the Well is set aside for ministering the Healing Grace of Jesus Christ, through the Holy Spirit, to all who come.

Perhaps a blind man should be seeking out their help for his own problems, his despairs and his hang-ups? How on earth did I get to work here? The answer would be found somewhere in the last twenty-six years, in a slow process of coming to terms with something which otherwise would have crushed me.

Going blind has been a gradual affair, too. It has not been the result of some accident or injury, but the creeping disease known as

16

retinitis pigmentosa, known in the eyesight business as RP. The effect of this degenerative complaint is to kill off, usually very slowly, the millions of nerve ends that go together to make up the retina—the light sensitive part at the back of the eye. The disease is medically incurable, starting at any time in life and working its way relentlessly onwards, until total blindness becomes an inevitable fact of life.

It is easy to imagine that such a disability should take life over completely, allowing the recipient to be re-allocated by society, if not by himself, as one of life's casualties, but the opposite seems to have happened. Somehow, I have been given a place of victory to live in—a place of peace and love; a place of truly abundant life, in which to live and have my being. How did that happen? Looking back over life so far is to look back over a switchback road, full of ups and downs, joys and tears, recognising that the worst times have been the times of greatest blessing.

It has been in the troughs that I have been able to get close to God, rather than on the peaks. It has been in the lowest places that my healing has come. Peering back into some of the harder times is far from painful nowadays, because many of those pits are now filled with the healing grace which is Jesus Christ, and that vision is a joyful one.

Again and again, God's promise comes back—His promise to be there when I need Him. He assures me that, whenever I pass through the waters, He will be with me; and through the rivers—they will not overwhelm me. When I am forced to walk through fire, I will not be burned; and the flame will not consume me. This is all because He is the Lord my God, the Holy One of Israel, my Saviour.

However, as I write this, I am only too well aware that there are many who are 'worse off' than myself, and who suffer greatly. There are also some who are quite surprised to discover my blindness, as they measure themselves to be better off than I am, after all. There are some whose pain is temporary, and some who seem to suffer continually. Some are in physical pain and some not, but where the rubber hits the road, as an American colleague once said, the real problem lies at the centre. If we strugglers can find what lies there, and it is usually our sufferings, then God will have a chance to heal us with His grace.

RP had no effect at all on my early years. For a boy, I had almost the perfect childhood. My dear father, a professional naval officer of considerable standing and ability, had remained in the Navy for many years after the Second World War. Thus it was that I spent lengthy stretches of time in Malta, a sort of temporary family home, where we could see the most of him.

Memories of those days are filled with beach picnics with my mother and sister, our father being away a great deal at sea; learning to roller skate on disused tennis courts, and children's parties on ships moored in the harbour. There were clear blue seas to swim in, under piercing azure skies; and harmless jellyfish, which provided an endless source of missiles, to assail family and friends with.

My first twelve years meant commuting between London and Malta, from school to paradise, from spoiling grandparents to spoiling summer holidays. Could anyone have wanted for more? My parents had always kept a house in Hampshire, rented out during our travels, and it was to there that I reluctantly returned at the end of our Mediterranean chapter. I use the word 'reluctantly' with care, as our English home really was home to me; it contained the security and stability that lies so comfortingly in childhood memories.

After a spell based back in Hampshire, when my father served at Portsmouth, we moved to a tiny village on the south Devon coast, to be within easy reach of Plymouth, where father was newly based. He seemed to be away at sea for ever and ever, and I missed him terribly. Thinking back to those days, I am not quite sure whether I missed him for his presence with us or for the wonderful times he organised for me: sailors' parties and officers' dinners, sailing trips, and just being around ships.

Although he was away so much of the time at sea, school holiday times—especially the summer ones—were filled with sailing and canoeing, yacht clubs, parties, and so on. Life travelled on into the early teenage years, in blissful ignorance of what was to come.

To try to recall now what it was like to see properly is to allow these fondest memories to drift up to the surface. They are brightly coloured pictures of rows of beached sailing boats along the sea-weedy yacht club shore line, with stays slapping gently against angled masts in the breeze. There are full-colour pictures of rolling green and wooded hillsides, sloping down to blue estuaries, and the tiny harbour, with vessels of all shapes, sizes and colours, resting at anchor.

Even now, I can count the trees along the shoreline and see the wing tips of the swans as they beat the water: a long line astern of dazzling white bodies, lifting and taking off in the evening light. They would come slapping down the river towards the sea, rippling pools spreading from their wing tips, like the oars of a university rowing club, as their feathers touched the still evening water.

There was the rowing boat tied up at the bottom of the estuary steps. Mother had dipped deep into her Post Office account for that boat. My elder sister (Carolyn) and I remember living in that boat more than we lived indoors. The pleasure it brought us was immeasurable.

Then there came the moments of high excitement, too. Sitting on the cliff edge, in the early dawn light, feet dangling into space, we would search the horizon for that big old, grey naval cruiser—the one bringing our much missed father, returning from a year's absence at sea. Then there were the two of us, flying down the cliff path to home, our feet skimming the rough path, and then the tarmac lane to the cottage. We had seen the ship. Father was on his way, and mother would have to know that he was here!

These were wonderful times: close to nature, and full of promise. Just around the corner, where the estuary poured into the sea, lay our beach—at least we always thought of it as being ours, somehow. This strip of half-sand, half-rock, was only twenty minutes' walk from the cottage, and much used by family and friends at every opportunity.

At each end of the sandy strip lay multitudes of tumbled rocks, crowded in together and raised up at crazy angles, smooth and sharp; high ridges and deep pools—the family race track. Carolyn and I would start at one end and race each other headlong across the tops of the boulders, an incredible feat of eye and foot co-ordination. Somehow, we never fell, never broke a bone, nor grazed a knee past easy mending. Rock racing was surely the sport of kings! One of the first things on my list of exciting things which will just have to be done when I get to heaven (after worship) is to go rock racing with Carolyn again. What sport we shall have!

It was not until I reached the age of fifteen or so that I began to notice any effect of the disease which by then had just begun to take hold. The earliest wondering came when stumbling over my words whilst reading aloud in the classroom. Bits of words began to go missing, much as they do when one is very tired. But it was enough to trouble me, largely because of classmates' guffaws which washed, drowningly, over a small boy covered in embarrassment without knowing why....

However, I managed to pass all the requisite examinations—except one. The subject of divinity, as it was then called, was far beyond me. Church life at home and chapel life at school were just there because they were there; they were family activities and school lessons—never fought against, merely endured.

I had decided by this time, having passed all my 'O' levels except the one about Christianity, that I really ought to follow my father's career. To go into the Navy would not have allowed a burgeoning adolescent his little bit of independence, so I opted for a life in the Royal Marines. This was the nearest I could get to being like my father, without copying him. At any rate, he had given me a fair taste of the naval life over the years, and I had enjoyed every second of it. By the time these interviews came around, I was wearing glasses and had, somewhere in the background, a suspicion that something was going wrong.

I was living with an almost permanently bruised nose. The poor thing was being regularly and unceremoniously shoved into school notice boards by so-called 'chums', who drew great delight from pushing the back of my head. They must all have thought this act of teasing to be hilarious but each amusing shove still lingers in my memory; not as a piece of unforgiveness, but as a hurt pain from long ago. I had given up shooting, too. This had been a well of endless pleasure—not killing animals, I should add, but punching little holes in targets a thousand yards away. The school rifle club had a reasonably competitive reputation on the circuit, and I had loved being part of that; it was something at which I was pretty good. But it had to go. Things were getting out of focus, and sometimes I was even hitting the wrong target. Graceful, albeit fairly devastating, withdrawal was the honourable thing to do, before I started letting the team down.

No amount of gentle and graceful truth telling from parents seemed to register through my own denial. Looking ahead to things being worse is never easy. Failing to get past the interview board for entry into the Royal Marines was put down, fairly and squarely, to the Board's suspicions of my failing sight, although I know now that there were other reasons. Short-sightedness, for that was all it seemed like in those days, was not one of them. For the time being, however, it would suffice as an excuse, but a new line of approach to life needed to be found.

If I could not follow father—then my uncles, perhaps? They were not gentlemen of the sea, but they were the next best thing: gentlemen of the countryside. Believing that I could be a surveyor—a land agent, as my uncles had been—I set off to London to grab some professional qualifications, and from there to seek my fortune in the world. At what seems now to be the very tender age of seventeen, and with a parental support promise of ten pounds per week, I packed my bags and set off for the city lights.

2

THE RIVER BANK

The College of Estate Management, Kensington—then an extra-mural part of London University—was a relatively happy stomping ground for two years of student pleasures. There were girl friends and parties, films to see and sights to visit and, as a top priority, there were opportunities to play guitar in a little rock 'n' roll band, around the club and the dance circuit. I had applied to the college, in the search for proper professional qualifications to become an estate manager. The rural life had always appealed and there was a good deal of family history in the field.

The old and respected family firm of chartered surveyors and estate agents still flourished down in the West Country in those far away times, and I was sure that they would welcome another family member into their bosom. At the time it seemed like the ideal career, and there was so much to look forward to. Although the threat of having to work hard for three whole years was far from appealing, as it must be for so many students, I fondled a daydream through the time in London, that dusty, grey and noisy city, that it would be a life of leaning on gateposts in beautiful places, chewing grass, watching lazy cows on lazy summer evenings, and contemplating the deeper meaning of life.

Even then, I dreamed of wide open spaces, rolling countryside, big skies, and endless time to explore the gap between my little existence and the masterful workings of the universe. But first there would be studies, exams and jobs to be attended to. It is staggering now to think how willingly I charged off into this sort of venture, without any concern about the future; any thought of how I might hold down a job, without any eyesight. At that age, there was no way of telling how fast the deterioration of vision would be, and some sort of living needed to be had from somewhere.

At any point in a degenerative cycle, it is only possible to believe that the future will be a continuation of today. How can anyone imagine what life will be like when there is nothing left, even if there is only a little to lose? Two years into the course, I was summarily ejected for failing exams—a disaster which, at the time, I put down to the struggle with text books. But it was more likely due to the wonders of the London social life, rather than the physical difficulties of wading through the mass of reading material placed before my sore eyes. Nor was it just the London scene. We travelled a lot to Scotland; without, I may say, the knowledge of worrying parents; and played our noisy music at dances and private parties all over the border country, and over on the Western Isles. It was wonderful fun, rumbling and banging up and down the length and breadth of the country, in a beaten up old Land Rover, our heads full of rock 'n' roll, and with no sense of responsibility about anything at all.

While studying to resit the exams, I acquired a trainee job with a local estate agent. But, after only a few months, I was devastated by a letter from the firm, outlining their view that I would never be able to succeed in that business, because my detail vision was simply not good enough. There were maps to read and contracts to pore over, not to mention levelling and measuring equipment in the field, which needed reading to the minutest accuracy. Sure, this had been harder for me to do than it was for my colleagues, but I thought I had done alright.

This shock, being unseen as it approached, threw me completely sideways. It was like being told, in the middle of a fabulous children's birthday party, that one's pet puppy had just been killed crossing the road. The surprise takes one's breath away. My reaction was to retreat, as fast as possible, into the great place of safety at the top of the Hampshire house— three floors up, in my bedroom. However, pushed and shoved by parental encouragement, off I went to another firm, for a second opinion, as important decisions were at stake. That firm came to the same conclusion.

Now what? Instead of a future in front of me, I now had a black hole. Instead of early mornings, buses to work, busy days and tired evenings, I now had little to get up for, nothing to do during the day, and only tears to make me sleep. Now, there were no other reasons for apparent failure. Bad eyesight had begun to get in the way of life.

Days and weeks and months drifted by while, in the depths of emotional unrest and hopelessness, I drove round and around the roundabout of possibilities, discovering that each and every exit in turn was a cul-de-sac. There was no way out, and it hurt. I began to spend more and more of the day shut up in my bedroom at the top of the house. It was a room with many womb-like qualities: secure, warm; and I was alone with thoughts when they came—and the struggle with emptiness when they did not.

Sitting on a wicker-seated upright chair, with one elbow on the window sill, staring down the garden at the waving trees and the woods beyond the bottom of the garden, the hours and days went by, round and round, offering up no easy solutions to anything.

It seems now, after many years of pondering over suffering of all kinds, and any possible reasons for it, that it may just be one of God's ways of gaining our attention, and capturing it in such a way that His messages for us can really get through. How I wish that I had had some inkling of this fact in those troubled times. Much of the ache in the heart would surely have been replaced by a glimpse of the wonder of God. But I was young and had no way to make my way. In my own experience, it has been in the times of greatest pain and deepest depression that God's voice has become almost audible; His questions and answers at their most vibrant. This time was no exception. It has always been in the depths that prayer has been most dramatically answered. His presence has never been more real than in the fiery pits and the lions' dens.

My first glimpse of this came at the age of nineteen or twenty. I was sitting on a river bank, chewing over the possibility of ending my own life. Quite how I was going to do that had not entered my head, but recalling the moment in the fields, a mile upstream from my parents' home in Hampshire, brings to mind some of Elijah's words, in a similar predicament. He, too, was running away, unable to face what was happening to him at the hands of the world. He was running towards God for sanctuary: I was just running around in circles. The great man himself went a day's journey into the desert. He came to a broom tree and, sitting down under it, he hoped and prayed that he might die.

"I have had enough, LORD," he said. "Take my life; I am no better than my ancestors."

I Kings 19:4b [NIV]

I felt that I had just about had enough, too. My first two choices of career had been denied me, and I was slipping into grief for what I considered to be loss of manhood. Declining eyesight was already beginning to rob me of most of the things which were so important to me at that age. I had stopped driving cars and had no hope left of ever owning one.

I actually passed my driving test at the second attempt, and was sometimes allowed to drive the family car. But one or two really close shaves were enough to put me off, and night driving was almost impossible. Reluctantly, I surrendered my greatest prize, and gave up driving altogether. After that, to invite a girl out for the evening meant her coming to collect me from home in her own car—when it surely should have been the other way round? That unhappy switch from what was considered 'normal' by all my friends was a real ego bender.

It had become impossible to conceive of having a decent career—in a sighted world—which might yield any sort of intellectual satisfaction. My parents did have a wonderful book which outlined just about every career which it was possible to take up. Not one of

26

them had any appeal. I do not think I quite realised, in those days, that all the jobs in the book needed a pair of working eyes. They just did not grab my attention at all.

Social events were fast turning into nightmares. Little accidents, of one sort or another, were making me feel stupid and inadequate in front of young ladies. I hated that. I should have been able to brush off such incidents with a nonchalant wave, a 'grown-up' sense of perspective, but each event disappeared down inside, like a great painful black lump, and it hurt. The young male ego and self-esteem was being torn to ribbons, with no prospect of life being anything different.

An hour or so went by, as I lay in the crook of a large tree root overhanging the stream. I had taken the family dog along for the walk and she was rushing up and down the shallow bit: snuffling, splashing and tail wagging; loving every moment of her freedom, and her place in the world. I suppose I should just have sat and shared in her pleasure, but I became angry instead, wishing I could be like her, with never a care in the world—but I could not be. I was seething with jealousy against her, venting many a foul word of venom in her ears as she paddled up and down the river, totally ignoring my frustration and inward emptiness.

Life seemed of little use to me. There was nothing I could do with it, except be hurt in it and by it, so I began to think of some manner of throwing it away. The decision to actually try something was never reached for, as the thoughts became more and more serious, a question popped up in the back of my mind, in a voice I have since learned to recognize.

"What is going to happen tomorrow?"

God was not answering my frustration and despair with healing, nor even some revelation about future directions, but with another question. Of course I had no idea of the answer, so chose the more sensible step of waiting until tomorrow to find out.

Throughout all the intervening years, the expectation of something new and exciting from God tomorrow has stayed with me. I am sure that allowing suffering is one of God's ways of gaining our attention and, many years after that time at the river bank, I found C.S. Lewis referring to pain as God's megaphone, when he wrote that, "God whispers to us in our conscience, speaks to us in our joys and shouts to us in our pain."

One message that seems to come through in suffering, time and time again, is God trying to tell us just who He is. So often we need to be reminded that God is God, the creator and sustainer of the universe, and that He is, after everything, in control. He knows what He is doing. He chose that early evening, under the river bank trees, to begin to teach me. There was no flash of light, no great revelation of truth, nor anything like that; He was just reminding me that He was around the place.

We need this reminding of God's complete supremacy, because it is so easy for us to ask, 'Why me?' Some of us have stepped out even further in our anger and bewilderment, and are shouting, 'How can you let this happen? How can you be so unfair?' Even at that age, I could have understood a little better that non-Christians would have to suffer in a fallen world, but why me? Why us nice guys? For the time being, one prayer would have to suffice: 'God, where are you?'

3

TIME TO FIGHT

I sat there for a long time on the river bank, my feet dangling a few inches above the tinkling waterflow. A strange question haunted me, over and over, like a misty feeling that lay just out of reach, too far to grasp hold of. Was there to be some divine purpose in all this? Anyway, what exactly is a divine purpose?

Long after the dew began to rise, long after it had soaked the seat of my jeans in the wet grass, and long after I had begun to shiver in the chill of the falling dusk, I climbed stiffly to my feet, setting off in the evening mist and dampness, back along the river towards home, wet and happy dog in tow. By the time we climbed back over the barbed wire fence that divided the garden from the riverside woods, I had quite made up my mind that God—and I still was not quite sure who He was—had a plan to use me. Some sort of supernatural influence had met me at the end of my road and swivelled me around to start back the other way. Whatever, or whoever, God really was, He surely would not waste time on me, unless He thought it to be a worthwhile venture! I certainly understood one thing, which has stayed with me ever since: I had such a lot to be thankful for. I had a wonderful home, with super parents, who represented some sort of unbreakable block of security—a concrete wall behind me, which could take the strain, whatever was to happen in the future. My dear mother had repeatedly reminded me, "Whatever happens, always remember that we are here."

I could be thankful, too, that there was no pressure to get out and make my own way; I was being allowed to find my own solutions at my own pace. If I were going to be thankful, then I could only find one person to be thankful to: God Almighty, whoever He was. It might also be that, through my own troubles, God might help me to be helpful towards other people. That sounds a pretty heroic thought for such a young man, but I have since understood the Cross to be the greatest 'compost heap' in the world. To offer our own sufferings at the foot of that Cross, for God to use for His own purposes, whatever they may be, allows Him to turn our experiences to His own use, for the healing of others.

To be able to sit alongside someone going through the same sort of suffering, knowing deep in our hearts what it feels like, and then to pray with them for their trust in Jesus, and that he would lead them through, is one of the most effective forms of prayer ministry I have known. Perhaps, in this way, many benefits and graces would come to others, by the grace of God, as a direct result of my own difficulties. I must admit that, even at the most frivolous level, praying with others — or even just thinking at home about others in trouble — does wonders, these days, for my own low times. Would He use me like that?

To my joy, I have since discovered another possible reason for my poor vision. It actually brings me closer to the Lord Jesus Christ himself. In those days, I was beginning to feel a deep sense of rejection — not by anyone in particular, but by the shape of society in general.

I was beginning to learn that this world we live in has steps to trip up or fall down; it has pavements and street tarmac the same colour; it has doorposts of virtually the same colour as the adjoining wall; it has grey railings on grey pavement edges, that arrive, head on, in the pit of the stomach, when one least expects them. Then there are grey lamp posts which lunge towards the unsuspecting passer-by. The world seems populated by people who leave empty glasses and coffee cups where they can be brushed off by an unwary elbow, and who send letters and bills which look like tiny ink blots on the paper.

The world, and the way it works, was designed by sighted folk for sighted folk, and each time an accident occurred, or a cry for help became necessary, I knew again that the people who run this world had not made allowances for me. I was just not one of them, and in the main (and, I felt at the time, probably from sheer ignorance) they were turning their backs on me. My dealings with God had a long way to go.

Such thoughts are vague embryos in a teenage mind, and easily set aside for more pressing needs. There were still decisions to be made about a road for the future. The Royal National Institute for the Blind had by now been informed — by my parents, I suppose — of the predicament I was in. I was to go to an assessment centre.

As ghastly as it may sound, the centre in Torquay was a real haven. Some three months in residence there were without a care in the world. I was being looked after in every way: fed, watered and exercised. Joy upon joy, I was allowed to spend extravagant amounts of time in a fishing boat, pulling up mackerel on the end of a line, as if there were no tomorrow. I was taught to type, for which I remain eternally grateful. They tried to teach me braille, and in this they failed dismally! I spent many hours in the carpentry shop — planing, turning and French polishing. After one of the longest, hottest and best summers in my memory, I went back home to Hampshire to await the verdict. They had looked, listened and watched, and had decided that, with a little application and good training, I could become a telephone switchboard operator.

With the greatest love and respect for those who earn their living in this way, I was flabbergasted. Was that all I could do? I wanted to use my brain, not my hands. I wanted to use my education — not just simply manage without it, as if it had not happened. I recoiled at the thought of being a 'disabled person' or a 'blind person'. I was ME! I was a perfectly normal chap who could not see very well, that was all!

My foot was stamping with outrage. Why should I be confined to the poorhouse? The feelings of being cross rose to irritation, then to frustration — and on to sheer fury. No way was I going to follow their advice. I rang them up in London.

31

"I don't care much for your suggestion." I must have sounded too offhand. "What is the most difficult thing for a blind person to do?"

The answer was 'computer programming'. I signed up straight away, not because I had the slightest interest in such matters, but just because the time had come to get up and fight! Various courses in computer programming, very little of which I actually understood, came my way in quick succession. Then I was off to Yorkshire for a successful interview for my first job. I had studied, and become very confused about, the arts of computer programming, yet here was a company wanting to employ me as a programmer.

One look at Yorkshire and I imagined that I had died and gone to heaven! I fell in love with cobbled side streets, packhorse tracks and stone cottages on heather-covered hillsides, black 'satanic mills', and brass bands. It was a wonderful place to be. Here, at last, was somewhere that gave me some security, in the knowledge of being wanted, and necessary to the company's present and future.

By this time, there were no thoughts left of God; no room in the young executive mind. The way ahead was open, and it was for me to force my way down it. I sank into the industrial history, the grandeur of the landscape and the relative harshness of the countryside, the dry humour and the native friendliness. This was a good place for a man to build his own future in. My need for living accommodation had been filled by a lady and her husband who lived in the town. Her Yorkshire cooking filled the inner man to completion. It was here that I met Ginnie. She had come over from Lincolnshire, to spend a weekend with her aunt, my landlady; returning a week later, to stay for longer. Within ten days we both knew that we were deeply in love, and that marriage would be the only solution. So, in 1969, we became one in the eyes of the Church and in the eyes of God.

We married a year after our first meeting, when Ginnie had completed her studies at the Royal College of Music. By now an accomplished pianist and singer, she was well on the way through a course at teacher training college. Her parents suggested we might get married after her studies had ended, but young love does not always wait for common sense!

We set up home in a tiny cottage nestling in the foothills of the Pennines, with the date 1634 carved into the stone lintel over the door. Here, in two old weavers' cottages knocked into one, there were wooden beams and rough plaster; damp walls and a leaking roof. There were sagging floorboards upstairs. The bedroom wardrobes leaned inwards, needing a wad of paper jammed between doors and frame to keep them closed. When the Pennine winter fell on us, with its usual vengeance, we climbed into the roof and handed down scooped-up buckets of snow, like a two-man chain gang, before it could melt and bring the bedroom ceiling down on our heads. It was absolute heaven. A mongrel bitch called Sally joined us from the RSPCA, and we settled down to start life together. We moved house around eighteen months later, because of my need to be nearer work without being able to drive. Then James, our first baby, began to take shape.

My office had been moved a further five miles or so up the road, beyond the reach of a simple bus route. So, with sadness at losing our falling-to-bits love nest, we set off to the nearby town and a standard suburban semi, with a small fraction of the character. At least it had central heating, and the roof was in one piece.

Within nine months of the move, I fell foul of the company's redundancy scheme. So, with four-week old James in tow, we arrived in Wales. Losing one's employment, with a pregnant wife to support, inside the first year of one's first mortgage, is not the best position to be in, from choice, but had I suspected for one moment that God's hand was here, shovelling us towards Wales, I would probably have denied Him for ever! Yet His hand was surely with us. I started a new and higher paid job the day my three months' severance pay ran out. I had applied to Lucas Industries, a large manufacturing concern making brakes for the car industry, and had been offered the job of systems manager. This was at least two grades above my position in Yorkshire, and had the pay to go with it. Was this a case of God taking care of His own? We managed to buy a house on a modern housing estate, with a good bus route to work, and there we settled in to start again.

The new job went well. Promotion came along, and with it came more and better furnishings, until I was able to say to myself: 'See? You're pretty good after all. You've become the youngest manager in the company, and have a good income for your age. You can build a good nest for the family—and all by the power of your own brain.' I was well satisfied with the way things were going and, two years into our life in Wales, along came Robert to share life with us. Our cup was not far off full.

At around this time, the local Vicar came to call. I invited him to return, to talk things out. There must have been some stirring, deep down in the spirit, still remaining from those unhappy Hampshire days. Looking back now at this episode, I can recognise the first beginnings of the battle to come.

"You try and convince me there really is a good God up there and I'll try and show you that there isn't." This challenge went unheeded and we never saw him again. Our semi-detached home on a close-knit housing estate began steadily to become more and more of a problem to us. The boys grew up, out of playpens into that typically boyish phase of argument, squabbling and in-fighting at which older parents laughed knowingly, while we struggled to keep the peace. Our neighbours on the one side objected to their noise as they rode their bikes up and down the pavement, and residents on the other side began to comment about Ginnie's piano playing—the volume rather than the quality. The first anxiety led to upset and argument, whilst the second led Ginnie to play less and less, until the piano was hardly heard in the house at all. The growing need for space and seclusion for the boys and for Ginnie eventually forced us out onto the streets on a house-hunting safari, up to our eyes in mortgage debt and feeling financially unsafe in the extreme.

Forge House seemed like heaven on earth. It is secluded, standing in its own grounds. The sheer size of it only really came home when decorating and gardening began. We had a whole acre to play with: fruit trees, a vegetable garden and what seemed like a farm full of lawns to be cut. In those days there was still enough vision left to sow, grow and harvest the large vegetable garden, and we revelled in the arm-stretching space which surrounded us.

One thrilling aspect of moving our lives to this paradise was that Ginnie could have her own music room: her own place with her own piano and her music. This was to be somewhere she could enjoy her music to her heart's content, without any fear of upsetting the neighbours. Robert, the younger of our two sons, had begun to learn the violin. A music room would be ideal for him, if only because it meant we could be out of earshot sometimes!

I did not realise it at the time, but seventeen years ago there was one large, potentially dangerous, problem looming. The house was sandwiched between the local church on the one hand and the Vicarage on the other! Was there no way God was going to allow me to escape His clutches? Had the nut fallen into the jaws of the crackers? Very soon, one evening after we had just about settled in, our next door neighbour (who later became a wonderful friend) turned up in the garden and introduced himself. On meetings like this with the local Vicar, one always has to say something about going to church, even if one does not particularly mean it, but I said something non-committal at that first meeting, and he went away happy.

A new house and garden; a new village, and lovely people next door—it seemed that we should make the effort to be part of this new community. The following Sunday saw us in church. What a welcome greeted us! We felt warm and accepted. The boys, still very young, were made a fuss of. Perhaps we would stay, but it would need thinking about. 'Commitment' is a big word. At the end of the month, we found a welcoming paragraph in the new parish magazine, reporting that we were 'long-standing Anglicans', a line that lacked somewhat in truth but, as we read it, we felt locked in a little more to the church. Perhaps the writer was more cunning than truthful, or perhaps God was getting His plans under way through him. In the words of the prophet Jeremiah:

The shepherds will have nowhere to flee, the leaders of the flock no place to escape!

Jeremiah 25:35 [NIV]

We began to go to church, each Sunday. The boys joined the choir. Every time we attended, I felt more a part of things; more a member of a new family—one which knew nothing of my battle to stay sighted, in a darkening and blurring world, and which therefore stayed clear of sympathetic noises. This was becoming a place of acceptance. I listened avidly to all the sermons, believing every word of them. I listened with growing pleasure to the Bible readings at the services, and tried to remember them. Hymn singing was easy—things had not changed since my schooldays, but now the words seemed worth listening to. They never had done so before.

Having descended, on my mother's side, from a long line of Anglican clergy, and having been brought up in the faith, I had always believed in the existence of God. He seemed to be a sort of benign influence: a force for good around the world, but never important enough to devote much time to. I learned much in those early years, and soon graduated to being a member of the Church Council. Here, I saw the running of the operation at first hand. It seemed a long way away from what, by this time, I knew of proper business practice. I would often come home from these meetings in a ball of fiery frustration.

What a blessing those days were. I was learning all the time! Ginnie became the choirmistress, and I formed a fund-raising group nicknamed 'The A Team', which had plenty of initial success. We organised bun fights and bazaars, raffles and suppers, and trips in coaches to visit other churches—all designed to raise money for the church, and all with some fruitfulness. Going to church services twice every Sunday all added to the feeling of being cemented into the organisation. I felt at home, and sought in my mind for deeper involvement.

Perhaps it is a natural part of being descended from the professional classes, as they used to be called, and perhaps it is a product of the public school system and doctrine, but my in-built inclination was to think that going deeper meant going upwards. To be more involved in the church would mean climbing the ladder. I had been promoted from the back pew to the grass cutting rota; from behind the mowing machine to the Council, and from sidesman to chief fund raiser. Now where? Almost unwittingly, I began to focus my gun sights on the pulpit, on the clergy, the pastor—the manager's job.

4

DEMOLITION

With the dreaded fortieth birthday looming on the horizon—the imaginary halfway point, when some men's minds so often drift longingly into the unreal realms of alternative career moves—I dreamed of becoming a clergyman. Was this what is known as a mid-life crisis?

I could readily see myself in a dog collar, receiving all the love and respect due to that position and, most importantly, being valued for my cerebral strengths rather than being doubted for my physical weaknesses. All the organizational and management skills which I had picked up over the years at Lucas would serve me well, and by this time my theology felt pretty sound. Well, it felt as sound as anyone else's. Little did I know!

Had I known then how the gracious Lord was going to turn my life upside down, change most if not all of my thinking, reverse most of my outlooks, and then pour blessings into my existence with such abundance, I would never have had the nerve to do what I did. There would have been no need. I applied for training for ordination in the Anglican Church. The family were more than supportive. The whole matter seemed a very safe option. I could carry on working for my living at the factory and have priesthood as a hobby on the side; such a disgraceful thought now, but I was starting to be dragged down by life's quicksands. It would have been a wonderful qualification for alternative employment, should I ever be in the place of losing my position with the company.

The thought of becoming a priest began to open up, like an all too welcome parachute. This redundancy threat was starting to loom and gather, too, like darkening storm clouds on life's horizon. Recession, with all its accompanying evils, was catching up on us at my place of work. A company that once prided itself on the security it offered its staff was now in the position of having redundancy programmes for them. This would be a good time to put in a backstop. Security could just be on the way. My own vicar was thrilled. He set about smoothing the path ahead with church committees, whose approval would have to be sought, as a first step. This done, the application went forward to the diocese, for the Bishop's approval, and I waited anxiously for the call to interview.

In no time at all, I was marching around the park at the rear of the Bishop's house, rehearsing the answers to the most likely questions. 'Why do you want to be ordained?' and, 'What do you feel you can offer the Church?'—these were the obvious ones. I wanted the replies to be unhesitatingly smooth and professional. The worst question would be, 'How will you manage church services with insufficient sight?' Hoping that the subject would not be raised, I resolved to say something to the effect that God would find a way if He wanted to. After an hour of kicking down brown, crinkled leaves, along dark, grey tarmac paths, around the rainy park, the appointed time arrived. In I went.

To my horror, the room was crowded. A large table filled the space from door to window. At the head of it, sat the imposing figure of the then Bishop. Along either side were ranged no fewer than eight good men and true, some clergy and some lay, with one empty chair—presumably left for me. I sat down in it, looking around as best I could, praying there were no wet leaves still sticking to my shoes! Happily, the Bishop, in all his scarlet, was well out of focus at the other end of the table, so his presence would not worry me. As for the rest, I had no idea who they were; as all their faces were blurred, I would never have recognised them. The main worry would be guessing which one was asking the questions. I would have to be looking fairly accurately in that direction when answering, so that it might appear much less obvious that I did not have a clue who was speaking! Without being able to see lip movements, nor even which particular face was turned towards me, it was becoming so important to pinpoint sound source direction. In this way I could pretend to look straight back at the right speaker, a technique I was still trying to master, knowing all the while that if I mis-guessed the direction, I would be answering the wrong person. Would that not look as though something were really wrong? To answer without looking into the face of the questioner seems so rude; it would not take them long to see the size of the problem.

These were the uncertainties that dogged my interview technique. All the pre-interview planning flew out of the window behind me. All that remained was sheer fear. The first enquiry came down the table like a naval broadside, despite all the preparation in the park.

"Could you please tell us all why you wish to be ordained?" Suddenly, I lost sight of them all. The vision which lay before me was that of a flock of vultures, crowding around a dying animal in the bush. This image quickly faded, only to be replaced by a vision of standing on the edge of a lake full of crocodiles, just waiting for me to jump! I will never know how I came through that forty minutes of third degree grilling. Surely their hearts were all in the right place, but what is received always outweighs what is given.

I know I got home somehow, faintly outraged at this being the kind of interview process—lots of imposing people bearing down on one single individual— which had been discarded by industry years before, as it never really got the best results. We had long ago opted for a more friendly and informal approach, to get the best out of interviewees. So what a lovely surprise it was, a fortnight later, to receive a letter, saying that the Bishop and his team had accepted, and would support, my application. Even if my motives were a bit doubtful, it seemed to me that God wanted this thing to happen anyway, so I looked forward with eagerness to the final hurdle: the National Board—three days of interview in my nearest theological college.

Here, the questions were going to be more searching; more

thorough. Two areas needed my attention—both to do with eyesight. It was not so much that I only had the little sight that I had at that time, but also the matter of losing the rest. How could I cope with the job from a practical viewpoint, and how could I tell people that there was indeed a good God up there somewhere?

This was, undeniably, the first time I began to seriously question the latter. Never before had it even dawned on me that God and a suffering world had anything to do with each other. God, after all, was a fairly remote sort of character to me in those days, and salvation was something that might happen at death if we are lucky, managing to catch God on a good day!

Surely, the national interviewers would want to examine me more closely on these things. So I enlisted the help of a friend to search the Scriptures on the question of eyesight. The very first thing that he came up with was quite earth-shattering, and a lesson I have never forgotten. It read:

The LORD said to him [Moses], "Who gave man his mouth? Who makes him deaf or mute? Who gives him sight or makes him blind? Is it not I, the LORD?"

Exodus 4:11 [NIV]

'Some friend', I thought! I did not want to know this at all; this was devastating. Here was a God to walk away from, not one to carry into the world. Here was a God who was directly connected with suffering and, what was more, apparently the author of it—or, at least, my bit! How could I say to people that there is a good God? He did not seem very good to me and, to make things far worse, it was not other people's suffering He might have caused; it was mine.

Was it God who had made me like this? If they ask me how I feel about bad vision, can I say that God does things like that? If they thought that I might go charging off into people's homes portraying Him in that fashion, they might think that everyone would leave the church! They would not tolerate that, and I would be out on my ear! Suddenly, this all became a bit too personal and complicated.

I resolved to bury my wondering as deeply as possible, just hoping it might never come to the surface again—not in the interviews, anyway.

So many years later, after so many trials and so many falls, God had to drive me down to my knees in front of Him, before He could begin to get through and to impose His sovereign will on me, my eyes, and the life that went with them.

The second area which needed my attention rose up and took over, almost as an anaesthetic to the first. I had, long before this, lost the ability to read anything but the largest print, so the Bible was a mass of greyish dots to me. The prayer book in common use looked to be the same unintelligible nonsense, so how was I to take a church service? I supposed the answer would be to learn it all off by heart. That solution would have to suffice for the interviews. Walking down the street was still a relatively safe occupation in those days, but there was no way to read the house numbers on gateways or doorposts, so visiting was going to be tough.

Various visits to partially sighted and blind clergy, around the country, did very little to boost my confidence, but it did present some reassurances that I could give the Board of Interview. If others could find a way, then surely I could. At least, I could show that I had tried to be practical.

The following summer, I packed a bag and set off, in fear and trembling, for the third and final grilling. A two-year process was coming to an end; I was really getting on the way. After supper, on that first evening at the national interviews, I met for coffee with three of the ten candidates, vowing to keep as quiet as possible. I wanted to see which way the flow was going to go, before being public with any views or thoughts about anything. There was going to be no slipping up at the last hurdle. The first one said, "I'm a travelling salesman, in ladies garments. I don't really care whether they accept me or not, because I still have my old job which I enjoy. I'm going to be pretty laid back about all this."

The second one said, "I want to save people from hell fire and damnation, but only those earning less than ten thousand a year. The others will all be lost, anyway."

The third one said, "I've come because I speak the Welsh language and my Bishop says he needs more of us in the Church."

Suddenly, my motives did not seem so awful after all. In fact I began to feel that I would be far more acceptable to any sensible interviewer than these three. The longer I thought about it, the safer I felt. Self-righteousness produces a great sense of false security. I could almost hear myself thinking, 'God, I thank you that I'm not like other men, robbers, evildoers, adulterers—or even like this tax collector. Or, more precisely, this travelling salesman.'

The leaders called for volunteers to read at the church services. I hid at the back, my mouth firmly closed, trying not to be too noticeable. Demonstrating my inability to read in public would be a black mark against me, I imagined. The remainder of those three days have become an unhappy and blurred memory of ineptitude, inadequate answering, and interview questioning which was often worse than the answers. They asked me to chair a meeting consisting of all the other candidates—as a test of chairmanship, presumably. The subject they asked me to introduce and discuss was 'litter'.

I was appalled. What about the need to spread the gospel? What about the pastoral care needs of a parish? At a push, I could even have accepted a discussion on fund-raising for the church; but litter? I could not believe it!

"Oh well," I remarked to Ginnie, as she drove me home, "I suppose the end justifies the means." I was completely sure of things to come. I knew I would pass the test; I knew I would be ordained, and that the next few years were organized. For the first time in many a year, I felt secure. Life would be a winning streak after all. There would be a set of buffers up along the track somewhere, but for now I was safe from crashing. Now there would be a sidetrack, should it be needed, in the nick of time. As my sight continued to deteriorate, so grew the certainty that the company would have to let me go at some future date—some time in the future that was coming closer every day. Here was my get-out. All that was needed now was a list of instructions on the training course, and the new life would begin. Excitement filled the house. For a week we waited: the lull before the storm. The bomb dropped out of a clear blue sky, destroying everything. The rejection letter hit the doormat, and my soul went through the floor.

Everything had been planned on this one being a success. 'Devastation' is not a powerful enough word: 'demolition' is nearer. I just went numb. Total, black misery swamped me. I had done the best I could. I had applied every skill and bit of knowledge I had. Best behaviour had oozed from every pore and I had done my utmost to sound reasonably intelligent. All that was left was to sit on the back doorstep and cry. Self-pity came in like a tidal wave. What was wrong with me? Was I being punished for something? If I were being punished, then had I not struggled enough? Was there going to be no end; was there no plan I could make that would secure life for me?

Moving from being fully sighted to being blind when, as in my case, the process takes many years, is not anything particularly life-threatening. I was well used to the decline. In itself, it would not be the end of the world. The cliff edge of life that had formed in front of me was one of insecurity—and insecurity of gigantic proportions, falling hundreds of feet to the jagged rocks of financial ruin below. Without failing sight, my future would carry on, just like anyone else's; but with it I knew that I would fall off the end of the road into a dark pit of financial loss, of lack of self worth, and I might just drag the three people I loved and lived with down as well. How could I secure a home for Ginnie? The expense of running Forge House and a car, let alone a family, was beyond a teacher's salary. With the best will in the world, she would not cope financially without some input from my own gainful employment. James and Robert would need help once they left school, and they wanted university education.

Everything a man should stand for was being tugged away from me, by events over which I had no control. The mists of uncertainty swirled around, building up pressures behind the eyes and bursting out in fits of bad humour and intolerance.

Autumn continued into winter. The days shortened. The longer the darkness outside, the longer the darkness inside, too. I felt that a trap had been set for me by fate, and the gate had slammed shut.

Plonked down on the path, among Ginnie's garden tubs—that was the only place to be. They had been so full of summer promise and now, as autumn came to an end, the plants were wilting and dying back, losing all their glory; dry twigs in the dripping rain. I felt quite at home with them. We had much in common with one another. Rejection came up in unrelenting waves, and I was just getting nowhere. In fact, I was right back again on that Hampshire river bank, with nowhere to go. Thirty years or so it had taken, but here I was, right back at the start line again.

"God, where are you, for heaven's sake?" That was my only prayer.

5

MIDNIGHT MASS

By the Christmas of that disastrous year, I had just about reached the bottom of the pit. This was one of those slimy-sided holes that take enormous amounts of energy to escape from—so much so that superhuman efforts often finish with a slide down to the bottom again. One step upwards led to two steps down, nearer and gradually nearer to the black ooze underneath, waiting to drown me in the final plunge.

Being forty one years old was not helping, either! It is often around this age that the male of the species starts to take stock of his surroundings, realising that he is about half way through his allotted span and things may have got a bit rutty. Certainly, I had run up a blind alley with nowhere to go. Firmly in the middle of this second adolescence, being ordained had seemed such a good move in career terms. Perhaps it would have been possible to go into pastoring a church full-time, if the money had been right; then again, perhaps not. At least there had been the possibility of having a new hobby—preaching, and organising things in my local church, which would have been a wonderful safety net to fall into when factory life got a bit too rough. It might have made my job more secure, too. Perhaps the company would have found it a little more difficult than usual to sack a priest on humanitarian grounds than they would someone else who could see well, and who did not have bad sight as an excuse for not pulling their weight as much as they should. It is much easier, these days, to see such conclusions as being the most appalling reasons for seeking ordination, and I would be thoroughly ashamed of them if it were not for the forgiving grace of God. They were very real at the time. Such thoughts and plans were like rope ladders being thrown down into the captive's pit; my only way out.

Some men look at their wives, and the boredom of their marriages, using that as a reason for altering course. Or, perhaps, they look in the mirror, wondering if they are still as attractive as they used to be. But as Ginnie and I were more in love than we were on our wedding day, the cause of my restlessness lay elsewhere. It was not to be found in dissatisfaction with the present, but in the insecurity of the future. I was coping fairly well with the demands of manufacturing industry on the eyesight—after all, I was still there—but, at the back of my mind, was the undeniable threat that I would one day lose much more sight, if not the whole lot. And who would find me acceptable then? How would I even begin to do things I did today, or yesterday, in a few years' time? Some sideways career move into a safer place at this juncture would have been a smart piece of insurance against the future. It would have been a way of reducing this awful feeling of inevitability that lived all day long at the back of my mind.

'It must be a bit like this during pregnancy,' I thought. 'If it's exciting, it's great; but, if not, there really isn't a lot that can be done. Unless some extraordinary step is taken, I would have this baby, whether I liked it or not!' More than anything in the world, I needed that extraordinary step, but had no idea what it might be. I needed out. Life was promising to go downhill all the way. With the ordination door firmly slammed in my face, what else was I to do? Where else was there to go, where a disability would not matter; where it would not affect the quality of my output, nor the level of my income? There was still the mortgage, and the thought of being the cause of losing our home was frightening. Then there were our sons' university careers. If I lost my job, I would fail them too. The happy days of local authority grants for further education which even remotely approached the expense of going to university had long since dwindled away. There would not be the money to support them. The list of possibilities had run out. All hope was replaced by despair. The more I tried to apply my brain to the search for some other future that would be physically possible, the deeper I slipped into the pit. I was a lemming running over a cliff, and there was absolutely nothing to be done about it.

Around that time, a friend told a joke about a parachutist whose canopy failed to open, and I remember missing the punchline entirely; I had such an affinity with the poor man. Somehow, though, there lay the feeling that there would be a safety net at the bottom. I longed to turn to the Scriptures for help, but only the vaguest of feelings were aroused: vague, but there nonetheless. It seemed that a lifebelt from the Psalms had been thrown towards me, and I longed to grasp it firmly, but my insufficient faith prevented it:

He lifted me out of the slimy pit, out of the mud and mire; he set my feet on a rock and gave me a firm place to stand.

Psalm 40:2 [NIV]

How this help would arrive I had no idea, but the falling had gone on long enough. Now was the time to check that the lifesaver was there, ready and waiting to catch me. The events of the next twenty-four hours were to prove the truth of this text in the most practical and unexpected of ways.

There is no-one like the God of Jeshurun, who rides on the heavens to help you and on the clouds in his majesty. The eternal God is your refuge, and underneath are the everlasting arms.

Deuteronomy 33:26-27a [NIV]

On the Sunday morning before Christmas, we went to worship in a local church (not our own) and the sermon lives on as one of the key turning points in my life. The vicar—the Reverend Paul Mainwaring, who later became a dear friend to me, said this at the end of his sermon:

"Just as Jesus was born at Christmas, so it is my prayer that one of you be born again this Christmastide."

Why was he talking to me? I could not see the pulpit, let alone the preacher, so he could have been addressing some other individual or, most likely, the congregation as a whole. Anyway, I took the comment as if he had thrown a spear from his lofty place and it had landed in my chest. How ridiculous! The remark would never have been for me; I did not even know the man.

On the way back to the house I mused a bit on this, because in those days I had absolutely no idea what the expression 'born again' meant. I remember just what happened. Ginnie and I had determined to go to 'Midnight Mass' in the church across the road the following evening. This is the service that all the local drinking fraternity stagger into, after the pubs close on Christmas Eve, but it always has a super atmosphere about it. It is a great time for saying 'happy Christmas' to lots of the congregation and, with great relief, to sneak cards to those thoughtful people who sent you one without being on your list!

As the service began, so I had started to pray. My prayer lasted for most of the service, beginning with the offering of such thoughts as, 'Look, I've managed and organised my life pretty well, up until now. Nice house, nice car, nice kids, nice wife. I've got on well at work too; no one gets as far as I have without being able to see properly.' The self-congratulation stuff went on for a while, but then it really hit me again that I had reached the blocked end of the street. Without someone else's help—someone who can control and manage things better than myself—I could just be running off the edge of a cliff without noticing the impending disaster, until it was too late.

Something had to change. Something was going to give at any moment. By now, the begging accelerator foot was flat on the floor, and the prayer engine was revving uncontrollably. I begged and begged the God Almighty to take the management load from my shoulders—the responsibility for my own life—and to change things to fit His planning, and not mine any more. The more I knew in the bottom of my heart that I would not be able to cope in the future, the more desperate the prayer became. The need to have someone else come and take over was going off in my chest like a nuclear chain reaction.

God answered in a way which changed everything for me—literally everything. The time for going up to the altar rail to receive the Eucharist had come so, to my annoyance, I had to break away from prayer and march up the aisle in a haze of boozy fumes coming from the man in front of me. I had almost lost the mood completely by the time I got there. The new sanctuary lights my fellow committee members were so pleased with were quite blinding, just as a rabbit is blinded by car headlights. So the struggle not to bump into anyone, coupled with the smell from Mr Best Bitter in front took away from me the prayer spirit I had been in. The moment seemed to have passed by. The bread came by, and the wine. Then it was time to start back down through the dazzling glare of the sanctuary searchlights.

In the moment I began to push up with my hands on the altar rail, a man came and stood in front of me, threw his arms around me and lifted me about three inches off the ground—or so I remember it. I did not have to open my eyes to know that he was there. I could feel him there. This is not quite as strange a sensation as it may seem because, even by then, I was learning to feel the presence of lamp posts and walls in the street before I smacked into them, most of the time. Using that sense, I simply did not have to open my eyes to know that he was there. At any rate, people do not hug other people without their knowing it!

When eventually I got my eyes open, there was no-one around. The priests were down at the other end, ministering to the long line of flock, and it could not have been one of them anyway, because they had their hands full with the administration of the sacrament. Back in the pews, the next hymn had started. Ginnie turned to me.

"What's the matter, darling?"

I shook my head to indicate that everything was OK, but a dam had broken inside. The tears that rolled down my face—the reason for her question—did not stop for the next seven days. God had come to take things over. The relief was overwhelming. The knowledge that God had come for me was certain and unmistakable.

Ginnie had bought me a Cliff Richard album for Christmas. I

had been a fan of his since my early teens, and this was a record of spiritual songs I had not heard before. The stereo did not get switched off that week. The songs were alive! The words were reflecting the contents of my straining heart: love, adoration, relief. I was free; free of the responsibility of making something out of my life; free of the burden of provision for the family. I tried to write down the sense of movement I had tripped over, almost by mistake, and certainly without any persuasion or education from someone else. I had gone from somewhere to somewhere else, and all I knew was that I had entered into a whole new life.

LOST PROPERTY

Where is this God I cannot feel
Or touch or taste, or hear or see?
I know I need Him, but what of
The host of things He wants from me?

This awesome God, this holiness,
This Father, supernatural King,
How can this God stand near to me
And risk being tainted by my sin?

And must I live in hope and fear
Of my eternal destiny?
Is my salvation just a need
In the empty spaces of philosophy?

And how do I approach the throne
Of grace, the day my Judge returns
And will I be ashamed of all
His groans and sighs at what He learns?

This shortening life provokes these thoughts
This trembling heart, this wondering soul.

Will God add up the rights and wrongs
And then exact His awesome toll?

But wait! My melancholic heart
Did you not see the reason why
The Father's Son came after you,
You apple of the Father's eye?

He came to wash your life with Blood;
He came to pay your judgement due;
He aches to be invited in
His righteousness to cover you.

The aching Christ is waiting still
Outside my heart, he waits; the King
Who longs for self to let him through,
Who longs his glorious gifts to bring.

A new heart held in outstretched hands,
Salvation, wholeness, these are they;
For faith and love and trust in him,
My crowns on that salvation day!

It seemed like the title was a good one; I knew now that I had
been quite lost before Christmas, but that now I belonged, somehow.
I had become like a slave, not owning myself any more—and not
responsible for everything in life. The slave master carried the
responsibility. I was a slave and had never felt so free. I had a new
boss and He was going to take care of everything. My poor old
logical mind could not control it; my trained mind could not analyse
it. I just had to accept it, because it was happening. I felt like a
caterpillar turning into a butterfly. He cannot explain the process to
us, either. He can only go through it.

Like Jonah, I had been tossed about by the waves and storms of
life, fear and struggling. His prayer on being saved reflected all my

reliefs. From inside the fish, Jonah prayed to the Lord his God. He said:

In my distress I called to the Lord, and he answered me. From the depths of the grave I called for help, and you listened to my cry. You hurled me into the deep, into the very heart of the seas, and the currents swirled about me; all your waves and breakers swept over me. I said, 'I have been banished from your sight; yet I will look again towards your holy temple.' The engulfing waters threatened me, the deep surrounded me; seaweed was wrapped around my head. To the roots of the mountains I sank down; the earth beneath barred me in forever. But you brought my life up from the pit, O Lord my God.

When my life was ebbing away, I remembered you, Lord, and my prayer rose to you, to your holy temple.

Those who cling to worthless idols forfeit the grace that could be theirs. But I, with a song of thanksgiving, will sacrifice to you. What I have vowed I will make good. Salvation comes from the Lord.

Jonah 2:1–8 [NIV]

Looking back at those early days, I need to record that there was one major change. Overnight, I went from a complete awareness of the existence of God to a complete awareness of his presence. In that presence I was being loved and accepted with a strength of feeling that had never before come to me from any human being. Day after day, these words were being repeated to me, and how much I needed to hear them.

You have stolen my heart, my sister, my bride; you have stolen my heart with one glance of your eyes, with one jewel of your necklace.... You are a garden locked up, my sister, my bride; you are a spring enclosed, a sealed fountain.

Song of Songs 4:9,12 [NIV]

If that is what being 'born again' means, then, boy, did I get it!

6

HARNHILL HEALING

Within three months things changed at work, too. The works manager was putting together a special team of people from different backgrounds of factory life, to take a hard look at the efficiencies and inefficiencies of one particular part of the business. There were accountants and toolmakers, planners, engineers and buyers, drawn from differing ranks of staff and management. To my great excitement, he wanted me to lead the team and head up the project. For almost six months I wallowed in my new job. I had been specially chosen, specially selected, much wanted. It felt good. Not only had I recently discovered that I was loved by a living God, I had now found out that I was loved by a living works manager as well! Little by little, over that glorious time, I began to rise back into self-esteem — such a valuable commodity, and yet so easily lost.

I still thank God for that time, in which He allowed me to settle down again, and to regain so much ground. What was more, part of the function of being a team leader was that it fell to me to make a monthly presentation to the management team, on progress to date and thoughts for future directions.

This meant being on my feet in front of a large number of interested parties, who probably knew the subject better than I did. I had to speak for an hour or so, relying to some extent on an overhead projector—but mostly on wits! I would put up the slides on the screen with a flourish, but I had little or no idea what was on them or, for that matter, to whom I was talking. The only way through was to remember that each slide was probably about such and such a subject—which I talked around for a while—and then pass on to the next one. I could still see enough in those days to recognise the individual shapes of blocks of writing, which appeared as grey patches when blown up by a projector. These changes in shape served as an aide memoire to help the flow of the lecture; tricks that no-one else knew about. God, and a good memory, stayed with me, and only once did I get it wrong.

During one of these lectures, a gentleman on the front row interrupted the flow of what I was saying, to ask a question. As soon as he spoke, I knew that the answer would be on the next overhead, and that if I started on that one now, before I reached the end of the current page, I would be lost. That was a risk too great to consider.

"If you would like to wait a moment, the answer is on the next slide, when I get to it." I thought that was quite a smart way out. Whoever the chap was, he accepted it gracefully enough. His face was just a blur, anyway. He could have been anyone, and I did not know his voice. At the end of the lecture, when all had gone, my friend the works manager sidled up and confided, "Well done. That's the first time I've ever heard anyone tell the Chairman of the Board of Directors to shut up!"

Meanwhile, back at the spiritual farm, things were not going as well as I had expected. A growing sense of loneliness crept over me. I had so much I wanted to say about Jesus, and no-one to say it to; so many questions, and no-one to ask. I looked around the congregation at church services in my mind's eye, and gave up trying. I felt a growing urge to get into the Bible and find out as much as I could about this new boss, this new kingdom I was in, but I could not read it. I wanted to listen to people talk about Jesus, but so few sermons did. I began to wander off to other churches of different denominations, in a fruitless search for something thirst-quenching, but found very little. I found churches which seemed as dead as doornails, and places where people just jumped up and down, waved a lot at God, and then went home.

I longed for someone to teach me about love and the power of the Cross, about the assurance of salvation and the power of Jesus' name. Somehow I knew—not from Scripture, and certainly not from theology—that a great exchange had taken place. Because of the Cross, Jesus had begun to exchange my sorrows for his joys, my sins for his acceptance, my curse for his blessings. He had begun to take away any chance of my eternal death, swapping it for his eternal life.

It had begun to dawn, slowly at first, that if the King had surrendered his own life to pay for mine, then I must surely be worth a fortune! Now I could get up in the mornings, look in the bathroom mirror, and say, "I feel like a million dollars!"

My heart jumped for joy at finding that one of the men on my team at work was one of these 'born again' Christians. I planned to sneak him off for a private meeting or two, to see what I could get from that source. To my dismay, he always seemed to be 'anti-' this or 'anti-' that, when all I really wanted to hear about was God, not how other people should or should not behave!

I had no inkling of what was going on behind the scenes. God was working on the problem of what to do with a newborn child, whose inability to read was preventing him from eating and drinking. Someone had noticed something and reported apparent changes in me, whatever they were, to Paul, the vicar who had preached the Sunday before Christmas on being-born again. One evening, there was a knock on the back door and in he walked. "You've changed. What's happened?"

The weeks of loneliness in this new place welled up inside. There was nothing for it but to burst into tears. Thus began many hours of sitting in each other's houses, just marvelling at the living Christ and his words and works in the world. How gracious he was, a busy parish priest, to spend so much time with this inquisitive spiritual child! During one prayer time together, in my imagination I saw a picture of two men sitting under a shady thorn tree, talking with each other, in a timeless atmosphere of peace. Was this an answer to prayer? Had God found me a prayer partner in Paul? This was what I had wanted all these months—another man to sit under a tree with, and to learn from. Some years later, after Paul had left the area and gone on to do other things for the Lord, I was to see that same picture again, but in a way that would alter my ministry life quite considerably. There was to be another man under another tree in another place: one who was to stay forever.

One day, quite out of the blue because we had never talked about my going blind, Paul asked me, "How would you like to go to a healing service?" I said "yes" like a shot, not because I dreamed anything might happen, but because this was a new part of a new scene—something more I had not yet touched.

By now it was August. High summer was upon us. Long, warm, sunny evenings were wrapping up each day. On such a day, at teatime, we set off together across the bridge from Wales to England. Throughout the journey we talked of God and His love, of His feelings for me and Paul, and for all the folk who roared past us on the motorway, as his old, rattling, red jalopy bumbled along in the slow lane. I remember thinking, 'If this is the sort of car that comes with ordination, it may be best to stay as I am!' I had no idea where we were going, and even less of an idea what we would find when we got there—but get there we eventually did.

This was to be my first visit to the Harnhill Centre of Christian Healing, at Harnhill Manor in the heart of the Cotswolds. The car swung round in front of some old farm buildings and we set off on foot, having left Paul's car (I was sighing with relief) in the car park. We headed towards the little church in the grounds at the rear of the main house. Someone on the staff soon turned us around, back to the farm buildings, explaining that the numbers now attending were such that they had had to move out from the church into the barn.

I had never before been in a worship situation outside a church building—but, what the heck! I was feeling brand new in the kingdom, so there were bound to be new freedoms. Anyway, Jesus was born in a barn, so it must be good enough for me to sing his praises in one! The music group were warming up as we found our seats. How refreshing it was to be without an organ or a piano! They sang a lot of songs from a book I had never heard of—called Mission Praise. I faltered through, not knowing a single one of them. At least I had found something I had been looking for: they were actually singing about Jesus! After quite a lot of that, the Reverend Hugh Kent (who was the Warden at that time) gave a talk. Lo and behold, that was about Jesus too. This was all music to my ears. My thirst was being met. Then—so soon—it was time to go.

They had sung about Jesus from their hearts. They had talked about him as one who really existed in the depths of their souls. That was that, until Paul grabbed my sleeve, pulling me back down onto my chair. "Wait," he whispered. "It's not over yet." Then the work began, and I was transfixed by the scene. They had sung about Jesus; they had spoken of Jesus; now they were doing his works! Members of the staff gathered in pairs, around the walls of the barn. People began to go to them, to ask for prayer. This time, Paul let me get to my feet, and I set off—walking slowly, so as not to bang into anyone or fall over a loose chair and make a fool of myself. I longed to be within earshot of what was going on. I suppose I should have been going forward for prayer, but nothing could have been further from my mind.

One thought would not leave my head—Jesus really was alive and working, albeit through people, but still working, nonetheless. Of course, I could not exactly see much, but I could surely hear the gentle prayers, the noises of release, the sighs of relief; the tears of freedom from bondage to illness, if not the illness itself. This was riveting stuff, and all done in tones of quietly whispered authority.

There had been no hype, no 'worked up' excitement, just an all-pervading sense of assurance and security in the love of God. I was transfixed by the atmosphere, by all that was going on, and by the overwhelming feeling that some thick love was filling the barn from end to end. On the journey home, Paul dropped into the conversation that not all the ministers had been clergy, neither were they all men. It was just as well I was sitting down, fastened in by a seat belt. The knowledge that non-clergy, and women, can minister God's healing grace into people's lives would not have been something to have told an old Anglican like me, had I been standing up! By the time we got back as far as the bridge, my mind was blowing apart.

"Can I do that, Paul?"

"Maybe, one day. It takes an awful lot of study and prayer and training, and you would need the Church to do some work on your life in a purifying sense, so that you become a sweet channel for the Lord. But the basic answer to your question is 'yes'." Poor old Paul was a little taken aback. He had set aside his whole evening to take me somewhere he believed I might begin on a road to healing—a road back to full eyesight. He had such high hopes and yet, sitting beside him in the passenger seat was an idiot, on whom it had not even begun to dawn that the evening had been for his benefit. How frustrated he must have been! But there would be other times of prayer; other occasions when Christians would pray for my eyes, adding to those who have prayed faithfully over the years. Some had just wanted to 'have a go' and most have longed to see me see again, but the prayers are not answered, at least not in the ways that they have wanted.

For His own reasons, which I do not pretend to understand, God has withheld His hand, giving me instead the time and the insight to pray for and minister to others, and to have the enormous privilege of being alongside other people as they share their aching lives in His presence. I have learned from Him that healing is not always the escape from suffering, but always provides the gift of peace as we pass through such times. And here I have found a thundering truth. If I love the Lord my God with all my heart and with all my strength, then I begin to love people, especially suffering people—almost automatically. Loving Him and loving others is the source of godly peace. Everything else begins to lose its importance.

To love God and to know Him is the centre-point of reality. If I cannot see God, then which of us is blind? If I cannot hear Him, then which of us is deaf? If I cannot walk with Jesus, then which of us is lame?

There were many times, over the following months, when Paul and I could be found sitting on the dining room floor, singing choruses or praying with each other across the kitchen table. They were happy days. The more choruses we sang, the more I wondered if I should play the guitar again. The tunes were simple; but the only guitar left over from those blissful student days in London was old—and hard to play, as fingers had stiffened from years of not playing.

I stared longingly into the windows of instrument shops, dreamed dreams of playing again, and was assailed with gorgeous sights of instruments I could not afford. On one of these sorties into the town I found a shop I had not seen for some time, and was quite enthralled by the vision of beauty that greeted me in the window. There, in the centre of the display, was a white angel of a guitar with an out-of-reach price tag, which tempted and tempted me to lust after it.

"Oh Lord," I whined, "I would so love to have that one, but I can't afford it. If you want me to play again and help others to worship you, then please could you find the money?" Two days later a letter arrived from the income tax inspector. It appeared that, owing to some miscalculation at Head Office, I had been overpaying tax for nearly two years. A cheque would shortly be on its way. I rushed back down to the music shop, to discover that the price of the instrument, a good solid case, a strap to go around my shoulders and a small amplifier, would amount to one pound less than the value of the incoming cheque.

The God who owns the cattle on a thousand hills, or perhaps the guitars in a thousand music shops, was going to let me have one! Many more evenings with Paul passed, and I began to seek strongly after the gifts of the Holy Spirit. Together, we had read about them in the Bible, but they had meant nothing. Apparently there were gifts of healings and miracles to come; words of knowledge about other people, and the wisdom to use those gifts—none of which I had experienced, as yet. If I had truly been baptised in the Holy Spirit, then where was the power? Much as I tried to persuade Paul to talk about the gifts, he would speak only of love: the love of a father for his children, and the love of a teenager filled with infatuation for another. Paul was teaching me to look for the love before looking for the miracle.

"You will see lots of sights; you will hear lots of things spoken," he would say, "but if you don't sense those things to be full of love, then they won't be full of God, either."

7

HEALING THE BLIND

Within the first year of this new existence, two people, of whom I had never before taken any notice, arrived in my life. Ann was introduced to me by my next door neighbour the vicar, and Sheila, from our church congregation, found her way to join us, too.

The three of us settled down to pray together—haltingly at first, but we soon began to get the hang of it. We were not too good at praying out loud in the beginning, let alone doing it in front of other people, but we kept on trying. We worried a bit about using the right words, as if that really mattered one jot to the Lord; and trust—the key ingredient we knew we wanted—came only slowly. In the back of our minds grew the certain feeling that we did not want the sick to be comforted—as went the prayer every Sunday morning—we wanted them to get better! Together we searched for people whom we knew to be unwell, and we prayed for their healing, unbeknownst to them. Often, we were quite amazed by the effects of those prayers. Our interest in those in trouble grew and grew. At a somewhat slower rate, our faith and trust began to lift as we watched God's gracious hand begin to move. Adding to the joy in those earliest days, was the wonderful discovery that good eyesight is not a prerequisite of good prayer; I was beginning to find my wings. We had a sense that a seed was beginning to grow. The hunger and thirst to know much more of the Church's ministry of healing and wholeness was causing an ever-increasing longing pain in that part of the heart which yearns for the things of God.

Avid reading is no substitute for good teaching, so who was there to ask? Who to go to? Who to listen to? Asking around did not seem to help much. Perhaps we were just asking the wrong people, as most viewed our requests for teaching with some bewilderment, or the raised eyebrows of ignorance and suspicion.

We had seen so many people recover from physical ailments, and we had had our theologies bent and battered by apparent failures but, to a much greater than a lesser extent, the power of prayer was becoming evident to us. We had to learn the hard way that this power is not something in ourselves that forces Almighty God to fulfil our wishes; to work miracles for us. Like so many others, we were a little frightened of American-style shouting at Satan, or ordering people out of their wheelchairs in the name of Jesus, and of the pastor who stands at the front of his congregation offering healing of sickness, as one would a plate of bacon and eggs.

These sorts of practices seemed to us, perhaps from Paul Mainwaring's teaching, to lack the sort of 'giving' love that is so needed by those who suffer. Where there is no love, there is no action of God. This 'power of prayer' is greatly misunderstood within the boundaries of the Christian Church, and sometimes leads to frustration and resentment among those who are not so familiar with prayer. One such angry remark to us was put this way: "The trouble with you people is that you think you've got some sort of hot line to God."

Happily, this is true! It is a gift from God the Holy Spirit to the Church itself. We all have it. We all have the ear of our loving Heavenly Father. The truth we were just beginning to discover was that prayer has enormous power when, and only when, it is directed into God's will for an individual situation. If our prayers are in line with His will for change to take place—then that change invariably happens. If I will His will, then He will. So, the real question that faced our small group of three committed Christians was this: how do we discover God's will in any particular situation?

High on the list of prayer priorities was the prayer: 'Lord, help us to know your will for this lady or gentleman, and then help us to unlock your will in them.' Words of knowledge about the root causes of dis-ease would often arrive as a result of this prayer and then be proved true in practice. Within a short time, we knew that we would also need oodles of divine grace to handle these words of knowledge, as some of them were often close to being dynamite. Sexual abuse in childhood, for example, is sometimes covered by a spirit of trauma, which lies over the memory of the events that took place. In an instance like this, the sudden pronouncement that the cause of the presenting problem had been discovered might cause total disbelief at the very least, and at worst a complete breakdown of family life. Indeed, one lady had related the story to me that she had 'gone forward for healing' for clinical depression only to be told, out loud in front of the congregation, that she had been abused by her father as a small child. Her remedy, it was then proclaimed, would be to return home and confront her father with this fact, of which she had no recollection, with her mother present, and that she and her mother should then forgive the father for his wrongdoing.

Dutifully following the advice she had been given by the elders, she confronted her parents, who were understandably horrified and began immediately to fall into the trap of distrust for one another. A year later, the parents were divorced. She had moved from having a gracious and loving father at home to not having one at all.

Even to this day, we hear of far too many people who are fearful of coming to the Well because of past hurts imposed on them by the Church, in the name of Jesus. These words are given to us in great trust by our Father in heaven, and we were learning to use them most carefully to guide prayer and ministry—and for no other reason. By carefully remembering each occasion when we thought we were right, and were later confirmed in our thinking, we began to notice that God was tending only to give us keys to the root causes of problems when He could draw on our previous experiences, or on our understanding of possible causes and effects.

We read somewhere, as a little example of this, that arthritis, or rather the pain waves that go along with arthritis, can in some cases be connected with the tensions of unforgiveness. Talking and listening to clients describing their lives, we often found rowing neighbours, or upsets at work, or relationship difficulties in the family life. Teaching about forgiveness, and taking the client through confession, repentance and forgiveness, often work absolute wonders for their good health. I make no claim that this is a medical fact; I simply state that healing often comes through forgiving others.

The need to know more about root causes and how to pray into them began to be of continuing concern for us. To find, with Jesus, the cause of upset in a client, then to sit and watch them walk out of it through prayer, is nothing short of exciting. It is truly miraculous. If only we could find, locked away somewhere in the depths of the Christian Church, those who would share their ministries in solid, Bible-based and not over-emotional ways, then we would have so much more to offer God for His use. We were just beginning to see that the relatively small numbers asking for prayer were just the tip of the iceberg, and the problems which we were faced with, to pray into, were of an everyday nature.

More training seemed vital. First-year medical students are not to do brain surgery; they have to qualify. We, too, wanted to 'go to school'. We wanted to move from the lowly position of 'interested amateur' to that of 'brain surgeon' in terms of our being used to minister to others. We felt the growing need to learn to see each person as a combination of spirit, mind and body, intended by God to work together in harmony with Himself, taught by the Scriptures and given new life through the Holy Spirit. We were fascinated by the possibility that to put those who were suffering from disorders back into harness with God, in the name of Jesus, might result in His peace flowing through spirit, into soul, and on into the body.

Healing through reconciliation was on the way, if only we could find it. Perhaps it was as an answer to prayer from such hopeful hearts that Paul Mainwaring turned up out of the blue one day, with literature about the courses and conferences at the Harnhill Centre for Christian Healing.

This education schedule was full of subjects of which we knew virtually nothing, and here was a dream come true; here were the right people, longing to share. They had famous speakers and not so famous ones, writers and doctors, pastors and psychiatrists—all shades of people, who were God-fearing and encouraging. We were washed away on a wave of enthusiasm.

Sadly, too, the slow realisation dawned that Wales was a hard place in which to minister and learn. We were to discover, from the Harnhill education days, that healing and wholeness were far more of an accepted part of church life in England than they were in the country in which God had placed us. Since then, I have had many a long conversation with members of English churches who have done nothing but add confirmation to this view. It might not be fair to suggest that healing and wholeness are at the centre of things across the Bristol Channel, but in Wales this most beautiful and loving ministry was almost unheard of at the depth we were finding it. A few charismatics understood that they should have the faith to lay hands on the sick and pray, but that was about the limit. Wales' development in this area was running about thirty years behind that of England.

We heard of discussions in fellowship groups which were deciding that any failure to receive physical healing was due entirely to lack of faith, and that being born again, meaning that the old life had gone and the new one had completely arrived, thus eliminated any need for memory healing. These ideas had almost died out elsewhere many years ago, and we were so concerned for present-day sufferers of all kinds—in churches that profess to copy Jesus, yet whose leaderships were so lacking in compassion and understanding of the human condition. If we were to be properly taught by the Church, and then offer this knowledge to use for God in Wales, we would be far from the centre of church life; we would be right on the extremity, held at arm's length in the hands of suspicion. Paul had found this scripture for us:

And so Jesus also suffered outside the city gate to make the people holy through his own blood.

Hebrews 13:12 [NIV]

With a wry smile, he added: "You know, the place of sacrifice is outside the city walls."

Rather than give up at the thought of the long struggle for acceptance to come, we waded in with gusto. For over two years, we made the one and a half hour journey into Gloucestershire once a month, never missing and eagerly anticipating the next trip. Each day was bathed in sunshine, or so our memories have it, and each day was filled with awe as we soaked up everything they had to teach us.

Early in this programme, we spent a day glued to the edges of our seats, absorbed in the wonder of a lecture discussing the use of the gifts of the Holy Spirit in everyday life—not just when in a ministry situation, but walking through life at large, with expectancy that good things may be given at any moment. It made such sense to us that God could do His work in people at any time, not only during church services; and in any situation, not only when He had been especially asked to perform.

At the end of a long and fascinating day, the speaker offered to pray with anyone who would like to approach the platform about anything that might have come up during the day. I had made it my business to sit very close to the front for the lecture, in order to miss as little as possible of the action. As the call for prayer was issued, I was nearly bowled over by the rush!

"Me first, me first!" cried a little voice inside, but by the time I was half on my feet there was no room at the platform. The speaker looked over the surrounding heads and down at me.

"Get up here and help, will you, Mike?"

My heart pounding, I leapt to my feet. 'Isn't this great!' I thought. 'Only a few months learning, and the great man knows me already!' He had called me by my name and it took two strides to reach the low platform. With heart thumping, I took the third step up to be with him, and my pride was dashed in the process. I was not yet needed for my great experience, nor for my wonderful theology; he knew my name because it was written in bold capitals on my conference name badge!

Before I had time to dwell on this apparent let-down, a lady was facing me, with her hands pushed into mine.

"What would you like me to pray about?" I asked her, tentatively.

"I've gone blind with glaucoma", she replied. "The doctors caught it too late and I've lost my sight."

This, I should know something about; this is my subject. I should be an expert at praying with blind people. That is my problem, after all. Here we go! I opened my mouth to pray. Nothing came out—absolutely nothing. I simply had no idea what to say, to her, to God, or to anyone else.

Should I insist that she forgive the doctors for missing the problem? Should I ask her if she really wanted healing? With all the state benefits around these days, had she realised the financial consequences of being healed? Should I say this? Should I tell her that?

As I stood there, in desperate uselessness, without a word passing my lips, the lady fell backwards into the arms of those waiting behind her. I panicked. That has really torn it! Was she ill? Had she had a heart attack? Should I shout for a doctor? Was it something I had done?

No time to decide; it was on to the next one and the one after that, until the crowd subsided and the blind lady was all but forgotten.

The following month, back at Harnhill on a completely different study day, I had to jump smartly sideways in the car park to avoid a blue Mini, which shot past my right elbow with a loud toot. It was the blind lady driving home! God had been fabulous and, to my intense relief, He had been fabulous despite my nearly getting in the way with puffed-up thoughts of self-importance, and my total lack of prayer skill. What a wonderful sight to see! Once she was blind and now she was driving again. We sat in the car and prayed: "Thank you, Lord, for all that you have done for her, and thank you for bringing your power so alive in front of us."

Theology was beginning to turn into practicality. Within a few days, at a different healing service elsewhere, a pastor had offered to pray prayers of healing for those who wanted it. A young married couple, who were carrying a baby in their arms, approached the front of the church and spoke to the pastor. The problem lay with the baby's eyes, and those present who saw the ministry which followed testified to a wonderful and most amazing healing.

Again, I had been led to a situation where the issue was healing of eyes. I tried thanksgiving prayer again, but the feelings of thankfulness for others were drying up quickly, as it dawned on me that the first two miracles I had seen outside our own prayer opportunities in Wales had been to do with blind people. God had been demonstrating to me that He has the power and the authority and the will to heal blindness, seemingly with no effort.

There was no great time of counselling, no years of background prayers of faithfulness, no hype, no nothing: just God working with His children on His own account. So, why not me? What was wrong with me, that God had seen fit to ignore the prayers of years? What great sin lay between us; what block did I have to His healing mercy?

I thought God was supposed to love us all equally, so where is my bit? Twice in quick succession, and right under my nose? Now I was getting angry with God. Healing those two right in my face seemed so downright unfair! Either this whole thing was a figment of the imagination after all, or there was a message here for me somewhere, but I was not in the mood to see it. I sat at home and cried, in front of the cross that hangs on the wall above my prayer desk.

"Lord, Lord, why have you forsaken me?" I could see, in my mind's eye, for the first time, a picture of my feelings of rejection and how I saw God. A blacksmith was pulling a strip of iron from the fire, beating it repeatedly with a hammer into some sort of shape, then returning it to the fire to burn again. Then he would repeat the process by withdrawing the half-formed shoe, and beating it once more. That was me. That was just what it was feeling like. Living proof that God heals blindness had been thrown in my face—but that kind of healing had not been given to me. Elation for those concerned, and praise to

70

God for doing these things, had disintegrated into screaming waves of rejection and doubt. God may have His purposes, but where was the love, or at least the bit of love that I needed?

If God is love, then God must be equal love to all. If this love was not being displayed, then perhaps God was not love as the Church had always taught me. Perhaps they were all wrong; perhaps they were all talking off the tops of their heads. Perhaps theology and practicality do not meet in the middle somewhere after all. No wonder, I supposed, I had been taught that turning theology into practical Christianity meant trying hard to be a better person, and that the love of God should then be manifested by doing good in the community, or other such good works. I was just beginning to see that practical theology is about God at work in might and power and enormous love for us, but that discovery was fading fast into a sea of disbelief.

The next few days were filled with tears of despair, and a steadily growing fellow-feeling for Job, that Old Testament character who felt, with a great deal of apparent justification, that he had been badly let down by God. I suppose that, like me, Job had more than his fair share of goodies in life, and was an upright man walking in the ways of the Lord, just as I had been trying to do. God allowed Satan to strip poor Job of his worldly goods and his family and friends, together with his health. He, too, railed at the Almighty, of whom he said:

"All was well with me, but he shattered me; he seized me by the neck and crushed me. He has made me his target; his archers surround me. Without pity, he pierces my kidneys and spills my gall on the ground."

Job 16:12–13 [NIV]

The response to suffering depicted in the words of Job suggested to me that God was grinding me into the dust, and I did not like it. Not once, but twice, the blacksmith in my picture had pulled me from the fire to beat me up, only to thrust my faith and trust back into the furnace. Only time would shape what God wanted from me, and I was not to know that, then.

71

Also, there was anger and rejection, and inner doubts that could not be voiced in the hearing of other Christians: just doubts that had to be lived with in the early hours, pondered and despaired over, wept over and drowned in the tears of grief that come with dying faith. Years later, I found this scripture:

See, it is I who created the blacksmith who fans the coals into flame and forges a weapon fit for its work. And it is I who have created the destroyer to work havoc....

Isaiah 54:16 [NIV]

I remembered, then, that Satan had been discussing my friend Job, in heaven with God, and the conversation had gone something like this: Satan had proposed that Job was a God-fearing and trusting man, a good servant to the Lord, but he wondered just how Job's faith would last if all his most precious belongings in life were to be removed from him. God had actually agreed to let Satan have him, to strip his life apart, so long as he stopped short of ending it. Towards the end of the story, Job had to face a similar question to mine, and he came through it into a whole new relationship with God; a fresh understanding of God in all His Glory.

Either God is in control, or He is not. Either He has complete authority, or He does not. Either He is in command of everything, or I am adrift in a sea of chaos. Either I accept His Sovereignty over me or I deny it. Either God knows what He is doing or He is not worth having as a God at all. Either God is God entirely or there is no such person. There seemed to be no middle ground, and I was having to learn where to take my stand.

8

TRANSPARENT SHIELDS

Meanwhile, there was still work to do at the factory, a home to run and a family to be part of. There were still two sons to encourage and to help on in the world. There was a garden to look after, lawns to cut and hedges to prune, but most of my waking hours were lost in frequent headaches and on-going indigestion, a sure sign that my soul was out of sorts with God.

The paradox was quite crushing: a loving heavenly Father, and a blind man He would not touch. Or was He touching me? Was there some point, some valid reason that I could hang on to, explaining my suffering? A real wrestling match with God was just beginning, and was to last right through my remaining years at work until, very near to emotional exhaustion, I finally gave in.

It seemed as though all the early promise of new life, given on Christmas Eve, had begun to fade away. The fresh excitement of life with a God Father, who really cared, and who had the will and the power to manage everything, was dwindling out of focus. The flat outlook of depression was coming back. Losing sight was not now the cause for this suffering; one sort of pain was being replaced by another. It seemed as though my Father God had His back to me. While I spent these months declining in faith and hope, it became clear that there is a paradox between the reality which I saw all around me and much of what the Church says today. The world, or at least the part that surrounded me in Wales, seemed full of suffering of every kind and is struggling, as I was, to see the possibility of a loving God. At one and the same time, the Church was affirming a loving God, but failing to connect Him with suffering at all. This apparent mismatch became easier to accept, as I began to find that there is no easy answer, no easy-to-grasp solution, that is in any way convincing to most of us.

In long days of seemingly endless wanderings about my mind (and the garden), I found myself staring back through history—a subject that I had always found fascinating. Here, one can find countless lives involved in great hardships and pain, yet there have been countless people who were ready, despite their suffering, to declare that there is indeed a loving Father-figure of God who watches over us and cares for us. How could this be? How could all those countless saints be so sickeningly joyful in the face of their agonies? Thousands have actually died rather than deny this loving God! How come? There seemed little sense in this at all, and no purpose for their pain. I had seen blurred images on television of Ethiopian children, bellies distended from malnutrition, and pictures of burned babies on the killing fields of Vietnam. I had heard many a radio programme describing the total degradation of human souls in the old South Africa and the Soviet bloc countries. How was I ever going to work out that there was a loving and eternal purpose in such things? If I could see the reason for suffering in all these others, I might be able to relate that discovery to my own blindness. It was a massive struggle, of well-nigh impossible magnitude, to take on board the suffering before all our eyes, as well as the Christian viewpoint of a caring, loving God.

How could I begin to say that there might be a purpose, let alone joy, in a suffering world? What could I say to the lady whose child was lost in a swimming accident, or to the mother whose son had committed suicide? What could possibly be said to the man who was in the seemingly unstoppable process of losing his sight? How was anyone going to convince me that God cares? How was anyone ever going to look at my lack of vision and believe in Christian healing? I concluded that, if there is a reason for all this, then it is far from being obvious. The answer was not jumping out of the woodwork. If, in the face of all this suffering, there are still many who would tell us that there is a God who looks down at all this reality and still loves us— the God who holds the whole world in His hands and, surprisingly, is actually in control of it all—then the purpose of suffering must be well hidden from view.

Then I wondered if all those who proclaim a loving God are deaf, blind and stupid, and quite incapable of looking the facts of life full in the face. There may be no answers to all these questions. I have not found one yet. But some sort of explanation would be well worth searching for, to gain some peace of mind. It may well be that we can do nothing at all about such things, and there may be many things that we are not supposed to do anything about, but there must be many matters that God does want us to address. I started on down this path of thought by searching for a true meaning for the word 'suffering'. In chatting around this question with those I met on Harnhill days, or with my lovely prayer partners, I had gained the distinct impression that suffering is something which other people have: not me, but other people.

I just have to put up with—and make the best of—what life hurls at me. I did not want to describe my own despair as suffering, for fear of elevating myself onto the same plane as someone whom I might perceive to be far worse off than I was. Had I not been brought up to put a brave face on things? I was thankful for the missionary Elizabeth Elliot, who came up with a definition during a recorded lecture that some kind discerning soul sent to me during this time of struggling. She said that she searched for a meaning for the word which would cover the whole range of suffering, from enduring a power cut when the family needs feeding to sitting at the bedside of a dying husband. In seeking for a definition that covers the whole gamut of human problems, she says this: "Suffering is having what you don't want or wanting what you don't have." I clapped with glee and relief at hearing this, because it included me as well as all those who were worse off than I was. Now, with a clear conscience, I could, at least, call myself a sufferer. Here was a label which did not display a need for pity. Here was a definition which allowed me to hurt. As all these thoughts tumbled and bumbled around like vegetable soup in my poor brain, I was still as determined as ever to learn about the deeper things of God—and the ministered results of this love— of which the Church continually reminded me, every time I went to Sunday services.

Doggedly, we returned to Harnhill for their Teaching Days; up and down the motorway, month after month, until the car could almost find its own way without a driver, and each time was as enthralling as the previous one.

Somehow, and probably by the grace of God, teachings about the healing of broken lives seemed to absorb away the soreness of my own struggle. Somehow, the idea that so many could lead much richer existences as a direct result of His healing light, became even more and more attractive. I was really feeling the onset of a calling to minister in this way, despite my own doubts and fears; despite my fight to sort out my own theology of suffering.

In those blessed times, we learned about the womb life and the effects of parental unrest, of difficult births and traumatic early years. We learned about damage caused in childhood by wartime evacuation (something that was to stand us in good stead in Wales); and we were taught about sexual abuse, and marriage difficulties; and of ministering to the dying and the bereaved. God had so much to offer His children, if only He could find people to work with Him; and He seemed to be calling us to help. The only problem was my own personal, hidden sorrow—that, whilst God could be so wonderful to some of His children, He was choosing to ignore my own need for healing.

Another form of darkening doubt was starting to creep in as we approached the end of that happy time at Harnhill. At face value, there was nothing that God could not do. Judging by all the lovely examples given by the speakers, from their own ministries, there were no limits to how much He would do, either. If this were all true, then

Christians would have no suffering at all. It could all be healed up and washed away in the blink of an eye, and where would that leave us?

I did not want to deny God the witnessed truth of what He was doing, but surely we cannot all be perfectly undamaged and all healed up, or we would all be like Jesus and then no-one would need him any more! I tried to imagine what it would be like to live in a world in which there was nothing we disliked. There would have to be no toothache, no supermarket queues, no weeds in the garden and no woes to dwell on. Again, I tried to think of a world which has in it only that which everyone wants. This life would have perfect weather, perfect jobs, perfect homes and perfect hair colour! Of course we could add to these things perfect husbands, perfect wives, perfect children and perfect happiness. I once heard Malcolm Muggeridge say, "Suppose you were able to eliminate all suffering; what a dreadful place the world would be! Everything that corrects the tendency of man to feel over-important and over-pleased with himself would disappear. He is bad enough now but he would become absolutely intolerable if he never suffered." This is surely true. To apply what Muggeridge was saying to my own faith, I had to remember that the greatest things I know about God have been given to me in my deepest moments of anxiety and despair. Not just in my own life, either. Some of the deepest lessons God has taught me have been given to me while listening to the stories of other people's lives and the agonies they have endured.

It is in the deepest waters, and the hottest fires, that the most profound things of God come through. It was just beginning to dawn on me that, if God can only really be heard at the deepest level in hot fires and deep waters, then perhaps that is why He allows such awful things to continue in the world. Perhaps our mountain top experiences are given for our joy, and the valley troughs for our learning. I was having to remember, as well, that there are times in all our lives when suffering actually comes to us through our gifts. Most precious to the majority of us would be wives, husbands, children and friends; and I am sure that one real way to avoid suffering is to remember not to love anybody. Avoid relationships and we can avoid grief. Stay away from the idea of having children and thus we can keep clear of acres of worry. To evade any form of friendship would save us from hurt and rejection.

A life avoiding any possibility of pain is a life of loneliness and despair. The gifts of love are often the gifts of suffering; indeed, the two things seem to be inseparable. God is love, but through love comes pain.

God, in His great wisdom, seemed to be playing with me like a cat enjoys a mouse. Even after all this time I was still smarting from being used in the healing of the blind lady, and I was still crying out with the unfairness of it all. Perhaps if He had used someone else it would have been easier to bear.

As I struggled on, with the now certain knowledge that love and pain come together—and that God and suffering come together—I could not accept this, in reality, for myself. The blacksmith was still hammering away, and I was hammering away too on the gates of Heaven.

"Why not me? You've proved to me without a shadow of doubt that you can do it, so what's wrong with me? Don't I deserve your love as much as the next person does? Why don't I qualify?"

Being given a gift of healing for someone else, and there not being one for me, seemed more like the unloving behaviour of the gods of ancient Greece, who played with men and women for fun, just to see what would happen. But, meeting me in my time of frustration, the true God, the Father of Jesus Christ, gave me this psalm:

> The LORD is my shepherd,
> I shall not be in want.
> He makes me lie down in green pastures,
> he leads me beside quiet waters,
> he restores my soul.
> He guides me in paths of righteousness
> for his name's sake.
>
> Psalm 23:1–3 [NIV]

It sometimes seems that God Himself is of little help while we are struggling to reconcile this idea of a loving God with the realities of suffering. On those intensely frustrating days, when I had to face up to the reality that I could not contribute to the family team effort by painting or weeding; or by checking the accounts; or driving the kids to parties, my prayers degenerated into demanding questions: "God, when are you going to get over here and do something about it?"

His answer was to remind me of Psalm 91, which says that if I dwell in the shelter of the Most High, then I will rest in the shadow of the Almighty. Perhaps I should be saying of the Lord, 'He is my refuge and my fortress, my God, in whom I trust. Surely He will save me from the fowler's snare and from any deadly pestilence.' I should be rightly expecting Him to cover me with His feathers; and under His wings I should be able to find refuge—His faithfulness being my shield and rampart. I would not fear the terror of night, nor the arrow that flies by day, nor the pestilence that stalks in the darkness called retinitis pigmentosa, nor the plague that destroys at midday. It may be that a thousand will fall at my side, ten thousand at my right hand, but it should not come near me.

My immediate reaction to this interpretation of the psalm was: "But it has come near me!" The pestilence that stalks in the darkness seemed a perfect description of the creeping growth of retinitis pigmentosa—the almost imperceptible effects of gradual death in the back of each eye. Psalm 91 seems to reflect a God who would not let bad things happen to us, for we are under His protection, but they most certainly and very obviously do! It seems, too, that when bad times befall us there are many occasions when God moves in His supreme power and heals the situation. Had the psalm suggested that thousands would be healed at my side by God's healing touch— but that it would not come near me—then it would have expressed my anger more closely.

Like so many others, I was left to ponder the question, 'If you really do love me, then why don't you come and help?' I cannot say that, through all this searching, I have received any intellectual answers to my questions; any logical explanations—nor any excuses from God. There is no intellectual answer; there is only a person, Jesus Christ, my Lord, my Saviour, and my God. There is, however, one path down which I have found peace—not a satisfying set of answers, just his peace. That path is the road which leads through the Cross. How sad I have become, in my old age, that the Cross is so despised by a suffering world, and yet I have seen that the Cross alone is the recipe for peace in life. This is far from being the negative sort of peace which is the absence of strife and war, but a positive driving force in its own right.

It is within the context of the Cross that, at last, I began to see that suffering and the love of God are reconciled. Only here do they stop being a contradiction, and start to harmonise with each other. They are the two sides of the same coin. It is on the Cross that the worst tragedy of suffering the world has ever known begins to turn into an enormous expression of the love of God. Even our own cries of, 'Why me?' or, 'Why not me?' when slightly re-worded, find their echo at the foot of the Cross. Spiritual leaders and thinkers of the time shouted mockingly at Jesus, "You healed others; heal yourself!"

Searching the scriptures for answers was a hard road without eyes working well enough to read, and I was entirely reliant on those occasions when we gathered together for prayer and study times, asking the odd question and hoping always that the right scriptures for me would pop up to help. Over and over again, I kept coming across the great paradox that, somehow, God is a shield under which we all live in some degree of safety, and yet suffering has touched not just me, but every family in the world.

Nowhere did I find this paradox expressed more obviously than in the Sermon on the Mount. Jesus wanted to teach us just how blessed we are when we know the meaning of sorrow; and that blessed, too, are the meek, who will inherit the earth. He remarked on the blessedness of those who suffer persecution, and how blessed we will be when people blame us for everything; mistreat and misunderstand us, and say all sorts of horrid things about us. Frankly, none of these statements made any sense to me at all until, almost as a by-product of the teachings at Harnhill, I began to recognise that there are two distinct worlds—one that I could walk around in, and almost see, and one that was invisible to mankind.

As my worldly vision was fading, so my sight into the spiritual world was clearing. As the mist thickened on earth, so it began to clear away in heaven. Things on another plane altogether were becoming more obvious and more understandable. I began to see that joy, happiness, healing and wholeness, peace and a settled heart, have very little to do with the actual absence of suffering. These things are found in the presence of God. Most people I have ever met seemed to suggest that the removal of all suffering creates these things automatically, but it is not true; it is the incoming presence of God in the human life and condition that produces these benefits, even in the deepest hardships.

The psalmist, in the valley of death, said that he would fear no evil. He did not say that he would ignore it or that it was not a reality for him. He simply said that he did not have to fear it. He knew, and I was just beginning to know and feel, that the whole world is crammed full of evil—being a battered, distorted and fallen place. The psalmist simply said that he would have no fear of the evil which surrounded him, because, "Thou art with me."

Whatever was going on in my life, whatever the trials and tribulations, the flares of anger and resentment, the throw-away thoughts of giving up, God was, unmistakably, with me. I fell in love with that wonderful chapter from Isaiah, full of the same promise, that when I pass through the waters, He will be with me. When I pass through the rivers, they will not sweep over me. When I walk through the fire, I will not be burned; the flames will not set me ablaze.

Within such strengthening words, God has not promised to keep me away from the flooding rivers or the raging fires, He simply promises to be there with me; to make sure that these things are not overwhelming. Why? Because He is the Lord, our God, the Holy One of Israel. But still there lingers the knowledge that Jesus could heal me by just thinking about it, and many who suffer to a greater or lesser degree than I do must surely suspect the same? All it would take would be one quick thought, one Godly 'brain wave' and all this could be over.

Regular visits to Harnhill over all those months were coming to an end, and I suppose they climaxed with an opportunity to meet Bishop Ban It Chiu, that most beloved child of God, who did me the honour of praying long and hard over the question of my sight. Eventually, after a long time of silence, he turned to me and said gently, "Mike, I feel that the Lord is saying that He doesn't have many disabled people in the healing ministry." Of course, my heart filled up with disappointment at this seemingly final pronouncement over the future of my eyes, but that simple statement from the Bishop was to be the great turning point in my spiritual growth.

I finally began to learn something about God that I had never really seen before. I began to see that God is God. God doesn't actually owe me any favours at all. It is He who is the Creator and Redeemer of the world. My business, as a Christian, is not to get what I can from Him nor even to get what I can from Him on behalf of others. My job, as a Christian, is to spend my life in worship of Him, and to continuously seek for ways to clean and polish my mirror, so that I may be a better reflection of His love and His glory; a clearer reflection of the Light of Christ. This would be work enough for a lifetime!

So, where did I get this idea from that—despite all the pain, anguish and agony which blanket the earth and blot out, from time to time, my own spiritual sight with self-pity—that there is such a person as a good God in all this mess? I have not been able to deduce it from looking at the facts, that is for sure. It could be argued that people like me just create a loving God in our own imaginations out of a desperate need for love and compassion which the world cannot give us, but I am just not clever enough to do that. I cannot create God. No, this is he who was the Word of God before the foundation of the world, suffering as a Lamb slain.

In this way, I was learning to see that God, in His greatness, has only really got one master plan in mind: the salvation of the world through the Cross of His Son, Jesus Christ. That plan is of an infinite complexity, as it involves every blade of grass under my feet, every hair on my head and every star in the heavens. It includes every note of birdsong in the morning, every cloud, and every raindrop in the afternoon. If such a God is allowing suffering to continue among His beloved ones, including me, despite all the prayers that our churches or our families can muster to the contrary, then there simply has to be a mighty, as yet unseen, purpose in it all, for the good of the world. By simple deduction, I could now see, along with those others who have been touched by suffering in some way, that His allowing it to continue must be part of this intricate plan to save the world.

Every Christian proclaims that Jesus is Lord of his or her life, but this may sometimes be a statement of relationship structure rather than submission. In surrendering our lives to God, we may surely expect to be remoulded into shapes which will fit more easily into His plan for the world. This fact is very sad, yet very true: nothing in this world re-shapes a character more than suffering.

God has created a world which contains pain in large quantities, and I have heard many a long debate on whether He is, therefore, the true author of suffering. No matter how hard I may search for the answer to that particular question, I am assured that God uses suffering to shout into our lives for His mysterious purposes.

But what are His exact purposes for me in this plan? I still have little or no idea and, if I did, I might well make a mess of it. But what I have learned to do is to say, "Lord, as my damaged eyes are still not healed, you must have a reason to use them in some way. Please let your will be done."

9

MOTHS THAT SPEAK

Praying for people is one thing; praying with them is quite another. Every time that Ann, Sheila and I met for prayer, there were always a few we needed to talk to God about. There were always friends with difficulties, and church colleagues, in hospital or ill at home. Never were we without fodder for the prayer list.

Putting into effect all that we had been learning over the months, on our Saturday trips to Harnhill, we were finding, to our great thrill, that 'things' were warming up. God had started to put more complex problems on our doorstep, and yet still people got better, or they seemed to improve much more quickly than one would have expected them to, under normal circumstances.

Of course, there were doubts about all this. Medically, folk improve at different rates anyway, so could all this just be the natural movement of things? We knew that God, in His mercy, has designed us humans to be full of all sorts of natural healing mechanisms, which combat illness. Whether it was these speeding up, or direct divine intervention, we could not, frankly, have cared less. It was just so lovely to see people on their feet again, both physically and emotionally. How God organizes the mechanics inside us is for Him to know, and for us to marvel at.

At the back of the church, we met Dorothy, limping to and from the church services, with a heavy wooden stick. She had been subjected to a hip replacement operation many years earlier, in the days before plastics were in common use. She was on the hospital waiting list, for the old joint to be refitted, as most of its mechanical parts were now too worn to cope, and were placing her in considerable pain again. Shuddering slightly, at the thought of this poor lady having a rusty metal hip, we prayed with her. The pain left within a few days. It transpired, from later X-rays, that the worn parts were like new!

A few weeks later, we heard on the church grapevine that Ellie, at the tender age of 73, had been found unconscious, on the floor of her flat, having collapsed two days earlier, with a kidney infection. Ann bought a bunch of flowers, and we set off to find her in hospital. She was too weak to leave her bed, or even to sit up to greet us, but how thrilled she was with the flowers! After the usual half-an-hour chat, I got up to say goodbye and leave. "Would you like us to pray a little with you before we go?" Ann asked her.

"Yes, please."

To our not inconsiderable shock, Ellie rang us only two days later, to say that she had returned home, much recovered and raring to go. Every healing was a lovely surprise. But there was a whole side of this prayer life that was missing. Just as I need God to listen to me, so we were feeling that we wanted to listen to others. Just as I need God to spend time with me, so we wanted to sit with sufferers of any kind, and help them to pour out their pains and sorrows at the foot of the Cross. We wanted to help in other ways, too. From our training, we knew that we could help, in love, with the bringing of sin to God—sin that might be blocking His mercy; and we knew that we should really be ministering directly, as Jesus has told us all to, so his Spirit might flow more freely.

How could we break out of remote prayer, into ministry? This became a huge issue with the three of us, but our church was not one readily open to the idea of lay people having anything but very rude theology, and there was no reason to trust us.

As a prayer group, we had been relegated to the dampness and coldness of the tiny room at the rear of the church hall, which had been serving as a junk room for many years. Little did anyone else know how that awful room glowed with the Light of Christ, as we prayed with him.

Holy frustration built and built. Requests for God to use us more openly and freely crept into every prayer evening. By the onset of our last winter in the little room at the back of the church hall, we were to be given one of those glorious visions, which come through created nature, that would lead to the start of a whole new ball game.

In those days, my wife Ginnie and I were much blessed by an English Springer spaniel bitch, called Katie. She was wild and energetic, and needed a great deal of exercise—in the forlorn hope of tiring her out! Without a lot of walking in the lanes, she would scramble under the garden fence and be away for hours, lying in wait outside the take-away in the village, or hunting far and wide for scraps—adventures that would lead to her eventual downfall. On one of those precious evenings, when the sun was setting and the phone lay silent, I took Katie up over the hill at the back of the house, and let her run. With the dog off the lead and rummaging along the hedgerows, I was left to pray, leaning on a nearby gatepost. Surely, God had not brought us all this way to leave us so under-used, facing another winter of cold and dripping damp in the back room. I could picture our little prayer cell in the church hall, and the picture was just too far from my idea of practical Holy Spirit led ministry, and the shining warmth of the love of Christ. In fact, the cold dampness, the being shut away, the feelings of being sidelined—this was a picture directly opposed to our longing for a secure and outreaching ministry. "Come on, Lord," I said out loud. "We need you to get things moving around here. So much has gone so well; so many are being helped. We need you to put us in a position to reach out with our hands and our love. You'll have to do it, as I don't know what to do and, even if I did, it's surprising how difficult it is to organise just about anything when you can't see what you're doing."

In the weeks leading up to that evening, I had been listening again, with growing interest, to a tape recording of the Book of Job from the Old Testament as, by this time, I was developing a real fellow feeling for the poor man. Many of the thoughts that had come during this study time seemed to flow towards me, over the gatepost I was leaning on, and to fill my mind with more positive things. It was becoming important to hang on to the question of what is, and what is not, 'good'. The freezing damp of the 'Black Hole of Calcutta', as I had begun to call our musty smelling prayer room, was not good. Losing my eyesight was not good, and all the fears for the future, my wage earning ability, my independence being lost—these were not good, either. But, what is 'good' anyway? Being plunged repeatedly into the blacksmith's fire certainly did not feel good! Adam and Eve clearly had a definition of what was good for them, which did not coincide with God's definition of the word. So—as they parted company with God—sin, death and suffering came into the world. Their definition of 'good' had led to disaster.

Nevertheless, questions remain. We have a God who loves His children enough to want only the best for them, and eventually to bring about their complete happiness and fulfilment—and who has all the authority to make these things happen.

As far as the Church had always taught me, God is all-seeing, all-knowing and all-powerful. If, then, we fall into bad times, as I was in real danger of doing, was it so wrong to reason either that God is not so loving after all; or that, perhaps, He does not have the power to change things? Another way in which such deep feelings were bubbling up came from hearing and feeling the age-old question, "Why me?" By now, I had plenty of experience of hearing about others being healed—and yet not me. This is so unfair! At least there must be a real God, or no-one would ask the question 'Why?' That question presupposes that there must be a mind behind what appears to be mindless. Without the acceptance of the reality of God, I could only put my misfortunes down to sheer 'bad luck'. Then, there was my friend, Job, whom we mentioned earlier. We recall that Job was a blameless man; a righteous man. In biblical times, the commonly held understanding was that a good man would be blessed, and an evil man would be punished. The story of Job's experiences turned all that upside down. Job lost everything. He lost his flocks and his herds, his servants and his home, his sons and daughters; and his relationship with his wife fell to an all-time low. By the time his health had left him as well, he sat on his ash heap in total silence for seven days, in anguish and pain, while his friends just sat around and watched.

When his dam burst inside, he expressed a sense of anger which was like that which had lived in me for years. All those thoughts, from that Hampshire river bank long ago, came rushing up to the surface again. Job asks, "Why was I not stillborn? Why did I not die before I came out of the womb? Why should the sufferer be born to see the light? Why is life given to men who find it so bitter?" These were never my words, but the emotions were all too familiar.

There seemed to be three paths I could have taken at this juncture. The first, just like Job at that point, was to realise fully that I had to do my business with God, and God alone. Another path might have been to dissociate God completely from the process of suffering, telling myself that He is not the cause of suffering, and does nothing about it. This would have been the easiest path to take as I had found it to be the predominant view of Christians and non-Christians alike. Logically, this path leads only to a remote God without compassion, or to no God at all. The third path, much favoured among Christians, would have been to attach all blame for suffering to Satan; the sufferer believing that he or she is under some form of satanic attack.

Interestingly, I discovered that, in the Book of Job, Satan was clearly operating a very nasty plan, but was being allowed to do so only under God's control, and within boundaries laid down by God. God was still in control, and was working out His purposes through Job's anguish. In support of this 'theory' that God is in control, even when things are going wrong, I discovered from the Acts of the Apostles that Jesus had instructed the early Christians to stay in Jerusalem until the Holy Spirit came, to give them the power to witness throughout the world. As I followed their story from memory, leaning more heavily now on the gatepost, it appeared that the tribulations and attacks and sufferings, which were heaped on them, drove them out into the world; which is exactly where He wanted them! God's purposes were fulfilled through their sufferings.

Paul, too, I remembered, seems fairly well convinced that God's will is sometimes accomplished through His control of Satan, and through not-so-nice things happening to us. I had found him writing in his second letter to the Corinthians that a thorn in his flesh had been given to him, a messenger of Satan, to torment him and to keep him from becoming conceited because of some surpassingly great revelations. Paul is accepting that the thorn was given to him by Satan—but in order to prevent him becoming over-conceited. I assume that Satan would very much want to see Paul getting too big for his boots; only God would have an interest in keeping him under control. God had worked through this. Satan had given the thorn. Paul was suffering. God's will was being accomplished through that suffering.

Job had gone on to express outrage at God; words which encompassed a number of my own emotions. I was still losing sight—more and more each day—and still a jobless future hung over the back of my neck. He had prayed along these lines: "Can't you take your eyes off me? Won't you leave me alone long enough to swallow my spit? You shaped me and made me and now you have turned to destroy me! You kneaded me like clay and now you are grinding me to a powder."

I was definitely being prepared, as were my two other prayer partners, through our prayers and study times and the glorious times of teaching. But, perhaps more than the other two, I was feeling ground down into dust—by not being able to pray with people; by the hammer blows of the blacksmith every time anyone got healed through prayer; and through the dreaded uncertainties of my own future, and that of my family. I knew, too, that I was probably the last person in the world whom anyone would hold up as a prime example of a Jesus miracle. I left the problem with Jesus, making a mental note to get back to him the next day on the subject, and collected up Katie the spaniel. The two of us set off back down the hill in the falling dusk. The prayer of Habakkuk the prophet followed us down the darkening lane.

How long, O LORD, must I call for help, but you do not listen? Or cry out to you, "Violence!" but you do not save? Why do you make me look at injustice? Why do you tolerate wrong? Destruction and violence are before me; there is strife, and conflict abounds.

Habakkuk 1:2–3 [NIV]

On the corner of the shed which backs onto our utility room at home, is an outside light, which Ginnie had put on so that I would see the steps down to the back door. This is not one of those bulkhead affairs, but one of the hanging variety, which protrudes out over the last few steps, just above head height. A spider had built a fine web across from the wall to the glass light bulb cover, a space of about four inches. There, in the centre of the web, brilliantly lit for all to see, sat a white moth. I slipped the lead from around Katie's neck and tried to open the back door, but I could not move. I could not leave the moth. This was the first time I had come near the feeling of having one's feet nailed to the ground. This poor moth had only been going about its normal, mothy business of flying around lights but, half way around, it had been caught in the net. He had not flown into it on purpose; he had just arrived there. He seemed quite at peace. There was no fighting to be free; no struggling at all, and absolutely no awareness that, at any moment, a large black spider could walk out at will and consume him. If there was such a thing as innocent complacency, then this moth had it in abundance. All was at peace, but I was feeling trapped for him. What was I supposed to do? Did this have a meaning for me, and, if so, what was it?

"Ginnie!" I shouted to her through the open window. "Come and look at this." She came out of the back door and went straight to the outside light. Lifting her hand in the air, she said, "This is what you must do." As she cut through the web with her hand, the moth came free: free to fly around the light, just as he had been created to do.

God had given a fresh vision; not a clear one, by any means, but the calling was obvious. Here was confirmation that He wanted me to set people free. His special requirement, as far as using me was concerned, was the freedom of those who are unaware of being trapped. There was no sense, here, that healing might be on the way for me; but the message was there to see. God wanted me to heal others—to set them free.

Going to work the following day was never going to be easy! I should have spent my day being super-productive for the company, charging around the factory, making good decisions with a quick mind, but this was not to be. Most of the day was spent staring out of the window, lost in wonder, love and praise and pondering on the detailed meaning which lay behind the picture of the moth. My ordered mind was getting in the way, searching for more pieces of the jigsaw, to fit into the framework.

I began to put all sorts of interpretations on the vision, and came up with all kinds of possibilities—all in my own strength. But I know, now, that God's 'pictures' are often vague on purpose; He wants us to work at them, through prayer and through watching. After all, they are foretastes of what He is going to do—not always detailed directions for our further action. Nonetheless, I needed a road to go down, which fitted the picture—even if a step by step plan was not going to be provided. What was more, it would have to be a plan that a sinner and a blind man could follow!

The answer came in conversations with Gill Day, a lady with whom I had had the joy of praying on a number of occasions, and whose experience in the ministry of healing and wholeness seemed to stretch back for ever. She graciously agreed to host a monthly prayer group in her Cardiff home, at which the moth 'picture' would be held up to the Lord, and at which we would simply wait for further enlightenment. This group was to consist of herself, the three of us at home, and Paul Mainwaring, that dear man who had led me to Jesus in the first place. Added to these five was a nurse, and a clergyman from Cardiff, and the group was formed. The seven of us sang choruses, gave thanks to God for His provision and mercy, and settled down to wait.

There were many tears, as the two pastors recognised their own congregations as 'moths'. Over that six months, there grew a deep feeling of communal sin: that we, along with the Christian churches in Wales, had become stuck, and that our lack of freedom in the Spirit was contracting our relationship with God; that our national aptitude for spiritual suspicion was holding back renewal, and revival, from the valleys. But the Holy Spirit swilled and swirled around Gill's sitting room, catching the seven of us up into a world above my own emotional aches and pains. Graciously, the key to our next step was given.

Of the many pictures and Bible texts that God shared with us at that time, most of which are still very close to my heart, there stands proud the vision of a large pair of longing hands, reaching down out of a cloudy sky towards the roof of my own home. Although the moth had started us off on our desperate search for the next obedient step, this instruction was too obvious to misinterpret in any way. There could be no pondering over that one! Jesus wanted to start work— not at the back of the church hall, after all, but in my house! Even so, being a cautious sort of a man, I did squeeze in a prayer for confirmation in the car, when going home that night! By this time, God was so determined that there would be no misunderstandings about His instructions, that He answered that prayer as well.

Only two days later, I sat down to watch Whicker's World on television, without having the slightest idea of the subject in hand. Through a 'Holy Spirit jolt' in the ribs, I switched on the video to record it—a seemingly pointless thing to do, as I had had every intention of watching it through. It was about Jackie Pullinger in Hong Kong, and her ministry to heroin addicts there. She was asked how she got started, and retold stories of enormous efforts that failed along the way. In the end, she related, everything started to happen— once she decided to share her own home with the addicts. That was it! That was my confirmation! Our home must be opened and shared, for God's use. I showed the videotape to the others, and they all agreed. We knew what we had to do.

Would we manage alright? Did we know enough? Were we ready? Faith is all about risk, and the real question was whether or not we trusted God. Another prayer of Habakkuk came to mind:

Yet I will rejoice in the LORD, I will be joyful in God my Saviour. The Sovereign LORD is my strength; he makes my feet like the feet of a deer, he enables me to go on the heights.

Habakkuk 3:18–19 [NIV]

One other vision from that Cardiff sitting room remains—as clear as a bell. In that picture, there were three of us: Ann, Sheila and myself, standing around a hospital operating theatre table, on which lay a skeleton. As we prayed, the bones became covered in flesh, and the flesh became clothed; the person then getting up to join the circle. As we looked again, there was another skeleton on the bed, and the process repeated itself. It seemed to me that this dream was about love: God's love, and the result of its sharing. It came to me that healing and wholeness would come to others, on a sort of carrier wave of this love, and that, through that healing, those people's love for God would turn, from being mere 'bones', into a wholesome relationship. This was the centre of all healing. In my thrill over that picture, I rushed back to the factory the next day, and found a Christian friend I had met there.

"I've had a dream," I told him, "and it's all about love!" He sighed forbearingly at me and settled down to listen, more out of charity than anything else. "I've found the answer," I went on. "All we have to do is love people with the true love of God, and then they will grow as channels of His love into the world. Then they will go out and love other people into being more whole channels for God's mercy, as well. Isn't that great?"

My friend sighed. "You're not actually going to try loving people, are you? You expect that to make things happen? You think others will react to that? How naive you young Christians are!"

By now, the winter was nearly over, and springtime was on the way. The birds were noisier in the early light, and the buds were swelling everywhere. God's creation was full of renewing promise, and we had a fresh road, too. We fixed a date, 1st March, a Friday evening about a fortnight hence, and prayed prayers of offering. This was to be God's time, to do with as He wished. We promised to try and be obedient to His words as we went along, and we surrendered the dining room to His pleasure, for as long as He wanted it— provided it was only one evening a week! How arrogant can one get? We suddenly realised that we had no means of letting anyone know that we had gone into business. There had been no time for publicity; but, then, Jesus did not use it, either. We made no phone calls and wrote no letters—not because we had any high-flown ideas about relying on and trusting in God; it was just that we did not allow any time for that sort of thing. The week before, we knew (or thought we did!) that no-one would come on our first Friday. We thought we would just be sitting there, like dummies. That last time of prayer together was a restless one. Sheila, one of the group, kept asking if the phone could be heard easily from my prayer room but, even when assured that it could, she was soon asking again. I was desperately trying to have us praying for the big night, but the question of the phone kept coming up. In the end, I gave up and said a loud AMEN. As I did so, the phone rang. It was a local church, asking us to visit them that weekend, and preach and minister to them. God had handed us our publicity on a plate. As the phone went back on the hook, we looked at each other, and said, "Wow!"

That Sunday night, I stood up in a little Baptist chapel, out in the country, and told them that Jesus loved them, and that he wanted the best for them—whatever the best might be, in his view of their lives. After the talk, I sat down, half-wondering what happens next in Baptist chapels I had never been in before, when the pastor asked, "Would you be prepared to minister to anyone who needs prayer?" I said that I would, but they looked a pretty healthy bunch to me! Within fifteen minutes, the carpet was covered with bodies, and one lady had a perennial throat irritation healed, while walking late into the proceedings. We were elated: God was fulfilling His promises to us.

10

SPITTING ANGER

That was the start. Over all the years since then, there has never been an open evening when nobody has come. Things were getting really serious and I longed, more and more, for my miracle. To see again would really put our little group on the map, and the needy would flood our way.

I went back to Harnhill, in search of my healing. Room seven at Harnhill Manor was used for a long time as the farm office, before Harnhill's conversion to being a healing centre, in 1986. It is large, for a single bedroom, but it doubles as a counselling room, with a small circle of armchairs and a coffee table in the middle of the room, and heavy oak beams running along the tops of the walls and across the ceiling. From one of these hangs a centre light, just low enough to catch the top of my head, every time I walk across the room; it never fails to remind me of its presence! A cross and a Bible on the mantlepiece set the tone. A small window gazes over the yellow gravel drive, as it circles around the house and then out across a lawn, which looks as if it once did service as a tennis court. All the way down the far length of the lawn is a wide rose bed which, they assure me, is a riot of colour in early summer. The colours I miss, but whenever I pass by on the way to the little church, to the rear of the main house, the sweet aromas serve to remind me of the incense of our prayer lives, as they must be to God. How delighted He must be, when His children come to talk with Him!

My first ever trip to room seven was a somewhat scary affair, although many happy and rewarding hours have passed, since then, in that room; hours of prayer and meditation on the wonder and the faithfulness of God. In the years that followed this first session, many people have followed in my footsteps—to sit there, and to pour out their deepest feelings, to laugh and cry; to weep for ruined lives; and to stand, amazed at the work of God within them, rebuilding them.

I was staying in the house for a Time Aside with Jesus week. Because of the many visits to Harnhill in the past, before this memorable occasion, there were very little or none of the usual feelings of dread anticipation at going astray in strange places, and knocking over, or into, everything that others avoid. By this time, some of the staff were becoming well known to me by their voices. Those whom I had come to know were aware of my visual shortcomings, if not some of the other sorts as well! All this provided a modicum of security to lean on. I had been persuaded, perhaps from some small portion of the teaching, that my sight might come back through prayer, if some block or other could be found and removed— some particular barrier, of which I was unaware, that might be preventing the mercy flow I was longing for.

Here was the first real possibility of being subjected to spiritual scrutiny by Christians who really know what they are doing. They know what they are talking about, and they are doing it in love. No condemnation: just love. These weeks occur at regular intervals, throughout the year, at Harnhill, and are wonderful times for soaking in new understandings about sin, and the sorts of wounds we all have, just as a result of living in this world with other people; and ties that we may have to places, people or ideas which may be holding us back from spiritual development.

The subject of sin has always been of interest, as so many Christians I have met seem to imagine that it is only something to do with naughty sex! As this sort of thing becomes more and more politically acceptable in the world, and in the Church, even the naughty sex principle is dying out. Anything goes. I could tell that this had become part of my religious upbringing, too. So often, on Sunday mornings, I have heard the words, "If we say we have no sin, we deceive ourselves and the truth is not in us", and, "Let us confess our sins to Almighty God...." without any feeling at all that I and sin had anything to do with each other. No personal wrongdoing ever crossed my horizon. No-one ever told me that sin is simply a generic term for everything in me that is not like Jesus. Good teaching on the subject is a great eye opener, especially in the realisation that all sin and all types of sin lie as barriers between us and God, filtering His grace, mercy and blessings, as they flow towards us. The real truth is that the warmth and light of God's love is always shining above the clouds. The earth sometimes falls under the shade of passing clouds, and often it is dark, as the face of the earth lies under its own shadow; but these shelterings alter the fact not one jot. The sun continuously shines. Filters I don't need!

Now the moment had arrived for two of the counsellors to spend time alone with me, and to minister to whatever God had brought up to the surface during the week. The times of teaching were over, and the information absorbed. The times for reflection had drifted by. Now I was ready for the action. The time had come, at last, for work to begin to restore my sight. I suppose I was a bit scared, because this was the first time that such ministry attention had ever been paid to me, and the thought of being faced by two questioning minds, for a couple of hours at a stretch, was more than daunting. This was to be the first time that anyone had dug into my life in any serious depth; this was the moment to take courage in both hands, and overcome all embarrassment, for some greater good which was, as yet, unseen.

To make things worse, the first object of which I caught sight, out of the corner of my right eye, was a lightish coloured box which was lying, threateningly, on the little coffee table. Sitting down in one of the armchairs, I nonchalantly stretched out to touch it—a throwaway gesture I often used to recognise items that caught my interest. Horrifyingly, it was a box of tissues! Still, I thought, we men don't cry too much, so the tissues are probably for the lady guests! On second thoughts, the tissues might well have been there just because the coffee table was. Coffee tables are the most devilish things, jumping out at blind people from nowhere, catching them off guard; biting chunks out of their shins. Even the thought of coffee tables is enough to bring tears to the eyes. Perhaps that was why the tissues were there? A correcting thought flashed by at speed — almost too quickly for me to grab. It was a simple statement, made by a Salvation Army Captain some months before, which I thought was lost in the depths of forgotten memories: "A man is not a man at all, until he has cried in the presence of the Lord."

Looking back over the acres of wonderfully healing hours that I have spent in that room, ministering to people, during the intervening years, when invited to join the counselling team, the lesson sails home again about how others must sometimes feel when faced with two seemingly holy people, and being so stuck for words for the first time. Well, not me; I was not aiming to be stuck for words!

Whilst others were graciously using their time to wait for the Holy Spirit to reveal things in their own lives that needed his healing touch, I had been stalking the country lanes in the sunshine, like Nelson on the quarterdeck, prodding the edge of the roadside bank with a walking stick, to make sure I stayed on the straight and narrow tarmac. I had been dredging up feelings from the past about this hurt and that pain, in readiness for the dreaded time of ministry; but all, in the end, to no avail.

There were plenty of memories to work on — there always are. Again, I raked over the still warm embers of hurt from schoolboy bullying, and many of those times when we feel the world is rejecting — and just not understanding how deeply sensitive, and misunderstood, we disabled people are! By this point in my walk through life with Jesus, I had heard story after story of the lasting damage caused to our personalities, which results from mistakes in parenting; or the dreadful things that teachers come out with sometimes, which affect our thought patterns and mind sets for the rest of our lives.

What about my parents? Had their parental inadequacies caused me to hold back from God? Did I have any tendency to cover a wounded heart in emotional ways, shading it from God's love in the process? If anything, the opposite was true. The good things that I had inherited from them far outweighed any not so good things. Was I a 'much misunderstood' child? No more than I would have expected from the generation gap between any child and his or her parents.

What about those in authority at school, or the attitude of playmates? Well, there were one or two memories that still hurt a little to think of. Perhaps I would hang on to them as fodder for my ministry session; but, then again, if they were just memories, and not great triggers of bad behaviour or thought patterns, I might lead my counsellors up the wrong path.

The more I walked and thought, the greater a muddle my memories became. Looking back, now, through the great healing times since then, and the greatly privileged times of being allowed to share in other folks' feelings of rejection, it is almost embarrassing to recall these thoughts. The uncomfortable truth is that disabled people are not necessarily any more sensitive, or damaged, or rejected than anyone else. The only difference is that the world is not really built for us, leaving us not so much with pictures of specific rejections in the foreground, but with the general background feeling that, despite everything that is said and done, we represent a nuisance value which the world could well do without. Those of us in wheelchairs are angry at the lack of ramps, but nothing seems designed for them; not cars, or boats, or planes, nor other people's houses, or anything much at all. Blind people suffer in just the same way over the questions of steps and all those other things, to which we may add newspapers, magazines, shop names and, to my despair, signs which hang in public and say 'GENTS'! As I have said, the world is designed by sighted people for sighted people. What this view of the world does is to invade our souls with waves of diminutive rejection. In a sense, the whole world, its design and its manner of operation, is 'anti us' and, oh, how easy it is to let the evil of self-pity leaden our souls!

It was in this week that I learned another lesson: that self-examination is rather like looking at one's own reflection in a mirror—the image is back to front. One usually finishes up with the wrong end of the stick altogether! This occasion was to prove the point: in the moment when all those perceived hurts flew out of the window, over the tennis court, and out across the Cotswold countryside. As Hugh Kent finished the opening prayer for the session, all my prepared thoughts flew away. I was left only with the overwhelming feeling that these two dear people, sitting opposite me, were about to interview me for a job. So, that is what I told them.

"How do you feel?" they asked.

"Just as if I'm being interviewed!" I wished, then, that I had said anything but the words that fell out, as they seemed so negative and so far from my planned speech. More than anything, I wanted to be out in the sunshine, on the tennis court, with the muffled clattering of the mowing machine. The scene that began to pour from my imagination, and out through my ever open mouth, was the interview board room at the Bishop's Palace, and then some stories from individual interviews at theological college.

The memories flared up, flashing past like a quickfire slide show. There, again, was the man who conducted my interview while stretched out on his bed, and the lady interviewer who assured me she did not like men, anyway. There, again, was the candidate who tried to convince us all that anyone earning over ten thousand pounds a year would never enter the Kingdom of Heaven. He said that he had come to this staggering conclusion after much prayer and meditation on the words of Jesus, when he explained to his disciples that it would be harder for a rich man to enter the Kingdom of Heaven than it would be for a camel to pass through the eye of a needle. One can only hope that God understands inflation! That little episode I had taken a bit too personally, as I was earning more than that at the time! Then there was that awful letter of rejection, with the pointed paragraph, assuring me that the decision was nothing to do with something they referred to as my 'disability'. I had told myself, a thousand times, that here lay the real reason for dismissing my application: they did not know how to handle it.

I was beginning to feel angry again. If I could handle my disability, then how come they could not? To my great shame, it all seemed to come swirling out on an uncontrolled waterfall of outrage. The more they listened, the worse I felt. Was I going on too long? Feeling that I might as well 'go for it', and get it all off my chest, I spilt the beans about my annoyances and frustrations—all of which seemed very justifiable and rational. "If that's the sort of candidate they get for ordination, and that's the sort of selection process they use, then no wonder the whole thing is such a mess!"

The more I pursued my theme, the deeper the hole I was digging. The more I talked, the more I realised, in myself, that all I was doing was presenting a huge lump of unforgiveness. What could they be thinking? What sort of a Christian did I look like? I had no way of telling their feelings, as I had no access to the expression on their faces. The seating arrangements were such that the two counsellors had their backs to the sunlight streaming in through the window behind them, which would have been bad enough if their faces had just been in shadow. At the point of sight deterioration reached that year, the effect of such background lighting was to remove their heads altogether from their shoulders. Their bodies were just vague blobs! There was to be no chance of picking up any body language here.

It seems strange to think of it now, but, up until that day, I had always found it so easy to see unforgiving thoughts in other people, but my own were never that. Mine were always rational, and quite understandable. Other people had unforgiveness; I had 'normal' reactions! Sure, I could get angry, cross, irritated and frustrated— but lacking in forgiveness? Not me! Other people could just be hurt children at heart, but my feelings were always those of the rational thinking adult. How blind can one get! 'The whole system is crazy,' I almost yelled at them. I thought, 'They haven't a clue how to go about selection. It's about time someone dragged them into the twentieth century!' I stopped, and waited for the onslaught of holy criticism over my attitude, but it never came. Instead of condemnation, I seemed to slip gently and quietly into an atmosphere of complete love and acceptance on their part. They did not discuss the rights and wrongs at all; they just came alongside me in my frustration and, with only a few minutes of my appointment left, Hugh prayed that, one day, I would find the path of forgiveness for what the Church, as I saw it then, had done to me.

Within five minutes, I was getting cross again, this time with myself. "Well, my friend," I whispered into my cupped hands, as I sat on the edge of the bed, in despair at the disappointment, "this time you've blown it. A whole week devoted to finding some blockages to your healing, and all you got was some seemingly vague prayer that you should do a bit of forgiving." I had behaved rather badly, and got nowhere. What a waste! I had begun to think that, if I had played my cards a little more gracefully, I might have gone home with my healing. Instead of that special moment, to take back to Ginnie, and to Wales, all I had were my thoughts, and the feeling that I must have looked awful, shallow and ungodly in front of a group of other people.

The words of Psalm 119 gave me the prayer I was looking for. "Oh Lord," I sighed, "my eyes fail, looking for your salvation, looking for your righteous promise." (cf. Psalm 119:123a [NIV]).

The bottom line, still hidden to me then, was that Almighty God does what He wants to do, and if that does not happen to coincide with what I want Him to do, He still goes ahead and fulfils His plans, and not mine. I was beginning to learn that God is God and not some supernatural force at the fingertips of certain chosen Christians.

The counsellors at Harnhill had found God's will for my week, and I had missed it. God, in His wisdom and for His purposes, which are well past my understanding, was wanting to deal with a forgiveness problem that lay directly between me and His chosen path. If I could have stared into a mirror that day, all that would have appeared would have been the image of a spoilt child.

The psalmist goes on with this great sense of surrender into God's will:

Deal with your servant according to your love and teach me your decrees.

Psalm 119:123b [NIV]

It is so difficult to explain to other Christians just how solid the barrier of unforgiveness is, to God's unfailing longing to help us in this life. This time at Harnhill was to open doors in a truly magnificent way. It was going to release others to come towards me.

11

LIFT UP MY EYES

It must have been well over two months later that the need to forgive really came home and, as I did so, God began to change things. What is more, He began with my relationship with the Church, the one place where my bitter sin of unforgiveness had lingered for so long.

Suddenly, one, two and then three local clergy began to take interest in the group's prayer life, in a way that was so new and reassuring. It was as though my forgiving had somehow released them to come near. The power of God to heal relationships through our forgiveness was manifesting itself in a very obvious way: a lesson I have never forgotten. Through the things they commented on, it seemed that they actually thought we were an OK bunch of guys after all!

After so many months of feeling 'on the outside', and barely tolerated, we began to feel a little more secure. One of these clergymen came to my home and was nothing short of thrilled by my stories of God's grace, and how much we were becoming dedicated to prayer, and the idea of ministry to others.

During this conversation, I plucked up the courage to say, "One day, we could have our own place, a place dedicated to Jesus; just a place for him to do what he wants to do—anything he likes, as long as it improves life for people who know that they need him."

"That'll take five years at least to get going," came the reply. "But don't give up; just keep praying for it, and if God wants to give it to you, He will."

When he left the house, I got down to a bit of serious talking to God who, after all, owns the cattle on a thousand hills. Someone had once said to me, "If you roll up your sleeves with God, He will roll them up with you." That was what I wanted to do.

"There's a place in your heart for us somewhere! You know where it is, and if you want us to have it, then please start preparing it." I talked to Him about this 'five years' business but, in His grace, I felt Him telling me that it would take three, and I had no reason to doubt Him. This is the God who outstrips our expectations over so many things; why not over this issue?

I typed out His promise on a card, stapling it to the inside of the lid of my briefcase. The card read, 'I covenant with the Lord God Almighty that I will serve Him and worship Him in a healing centre in three years.' In the bottom corner, I wrote the date of the first evening, in the dining room at home, when our hopes and aspirations were so high: the evening when we came out of the 'Black Hole of Calcutta' at the back of the church hall, and began the offering of our ministry to God—March 1st 1990.

By now, the dining room had become too small comfortably to contain the numbers of people who turned up in search of God's grace. Mostly, they came with purely physical complaints, which are always the easiest things to pray for, and we were bowled over by the freshness of each miracle. I am sure that some were not touched, during the time that we knew them, but the lame really did walk again, and the deaf really did begin to hear better.

Before many months had passed, we were having to commandeer every chair in the house, cramming them around the walls of the dining room; leaving not even enough room to swing a guitar in. We began to joke, among ourselves, that at least people in wheelchairs brought their own seats with them. Even so, some were left to sit on the floor and the fireside hobs. What could we do about space? One local parish vicar took pity, offering us the use of his church hall for two evenings a week, for a small financial retainer. We enjoyed the increased space to move in. There were plenty of chairs to sit on, and no carpet to be stained with oil spots. But there were two mighty disadvantages to our new home. The facilities were abominable. There were no kitchen arrangements—just a power point for a kettle. The single outside lavatory would not have been out of place in a museum of nineteenth century social history! The building was situated quite close to the nearby canal, now largely disused, and the village river rats took it upon themselves to nest under the floorboards. Hopefully, there was enough worship going on to cover their scratching, but the quiet moments were a different kettle of fish altogether. There were many times when startled 'clients' had to be quickly reassured that the noises were only birds building their nests in the eaves!

In the end, we had to leave the rural life, and retreat to the rooms adjoining the local Methodist church, which the minister had graciously allowed us to borrow—but only for a short while. Here we met Postman Pat. This colourful chap was a large transfer, stuck on the window of the church children's playroom—the room we used for healing services. The heat of the summer sun, pouring through the glass, had melted his face, collapsing the whole of the front of his head down onto neck and chest. Hardly a picture of Christian healing! We cunningly arranged the chairs, so that everyone had their backs to poor Postman Pat, who, we hoped, would not suffer too much from the rejection in his hour of need! But at least there were no rats. Cross-denominational conjugal living is never easy. We began to hunt seriously for a place of our own. Those were happy times, though. We were roughing it for the Lord, and we really did not mind one bit. To look back at our two homes, one shared with the rats and the other with Postman Pat, is to see those days through rose-tinted spectacles; the rose colouring being provided by the answers to prayer, that filled life to the 'overflow pipe'.

In all those months, I rarely questioned my own missing healing. With all that there was to learn and experience from a real God, who actually does move in our lives, there remained little time to ponder on my own shortcomings. Towards the end of our time at the Methodist church, a young local lad came to one of our open evenings, and mentioned that an old chapel in the town had a 'For

Sale' sign over the door. It had been empty for a number of years, and was nearly derelict, but he thought it might make a good healing centre. We went, we saw; and we lost courage, at the state of it. But God seemed to have left it there just for us, so we set about the legal wrangling to acquire it.

My heart was not exactly leaping for joy at this point. We were about to exchange scratching rats and dripping postmen for spiders and rotten floorboards. Would all this ever come right? But at least the old chapel had all the potential we needed. A large main room would do well enough for conferences, and the side rooms were sufficient to provide two quiet ministry rooms, and a little self-contained chapel in-house. Across the back of the building, the facilities were to be found: there were gents' and ladies' loos, and a kitchen which, given a lot of work, could be made large enough to eat in. Above all, it would be all ours. We could be free to come and go as we pleased: able to arrange for people to come by appointment, and no longer in competition with any other activity. It was filthy, but it was wonderful!

Day after day, month after month, I went back into the factory every morning. Each day, as I collapsed unhappily and unwillingly into my chair at 7.15 a.m., with the first of many cups of coffee, I opened the briefcase lid, and reached for the card. "Thank you, Lord, for fulfilling your promise to me."

Each day in the factory began in that exact same way, but most of them soon deteriorated until, each evening, I knew that I could not take too much more. The pressure was on. The recession had arrived, and I had escaped the first wave of staff redundancies, by the skin of my teeth. All the months up until the second wave of sackings came crashing down on us, I lived in abject fear, knowing that I was not performing with the same competitive energy that others could muster. My sight had really begun to fail fast. God's message was struggling to get through, and I could not tolerate the thoughts that He placed in my mind. 'Give up? Don't be silly; there's no way we could afford that!' As the last two years drifted past in an agony of trembling financial fear—the two years that we battled with the rats, and the disintegrating postmen of Methodist back rooms—I found myself spending more and more time in the office in prayer—hoping that God was still there in support, but doubting every positive thought.

As the storm clouds of redundancy threatened again, I reached the end of the trail. Ginnie was in full agreement. She had watched me slipping and sliding down the slope of despair; the speed increasing as my sight went downhill and I could not cope with the work any longer. Surely, I would have to go. Ginnie encouraged and supported me, on and on, until the Lord finally showed His hand. The card in the briefcase lid had kept me going for two years, and a place had at last been found.

My lovely heavenly Father was true to His word. On March 1st, 1993, exactly three years to the day, just as He had promised, we opened the doors of the Well Centre, and I left the factory behind for ever. A lady friend of Ginnie's presented me with a paperweight, as a sort of housewarming gift, to sit on my new desk in my new office. On the top of it is inscribed:

You did not choose me, but I chose you and appointed you to go and bear fruit—fruit that will last. Then the Father will give you whatever you ask in my name.

John 15:16 [NIV]

The great day had come. The Well Centre opened. I suppose we could have had a band, lots of flags and a press launch, but I could not remember Jesus' ministry beginning like that, so we did not try. If this was to be the ministry of availability, then we would just sit, and pray, and wait. My last few weeks in the factory had been largely absorbed in financial planning—and there was no way that we were going to make it! I pored over the figures, with a strong magnifying glass, until the tears came to my eyes, but I could not make any reasonable sense of them. Everywhere I looked, the red outweighed the black. We had promised, and committed, resources which we simply did not have. I have never felt so downright irresponsible in my whole life. Waiting at home was an overbearing mortgage, that seemed to have a voracious appetite; gas and electricity bills, and—perhaps even worse—there were two young men straining at the leash to get through university, which would be impossible without parental aid. Perhaps I was going crazy. There were no guarantees here at all. I was committed to the Well, with no gainful employment, and consequently with no understanding of my income.

One thought kept pounding away in my head, drowning out the doubts and fears. Something good was going to happen— tomorrow. How that goodness would show itself, I did not appreciate at the time. I imagined that it was something very healing: some vague understanding—vague, but real enough—that God was going to assure me of something very much better than I had ever had before. But it was not just the financial argument which had to be surrendered. The frustration, the anxiety and the creeping sense of insecurity—all had to be offered up. At the peak of the emotional battle, God's words were quite clear:

"I want you to give up working for me, and start working with me."

Since those frightening days, I have discovered Hebrews 11:13, which illuminated, for me, this balance between the agony of indecision I was facing, and the knowledge that there was so much to come. The writer of Hebrews had been talking about all those patriarchs who had gone forward into the unknown, for no other reason than that they knew by faith that they had to. He writes that all these people were still living by faith when they died. They did not receive the things promised; they only saw them, and welcomed them from a distance. They admitted that they were aliens and strangers on earth. That particular extract from Hebrews goes on to discuss Moses in this light. He regarded disgrace for the sake of Christ (analogous, in my case, to holding the title 'disabled') as of greater value than the treasures of Egypt, because he was looking ahead to his reward. It was through his faith that he left Egypt, not fearing the king's anger. He persevered, because he saw Him who is invisible.

This sort of person seemed to have had a transfigured perspective on life. All things seem to have been just a part of their walk with

God, towards some unseen and greater goal. Their eyes were up, and over the horizon. The whole basis of my insecurity had been failing sight. Now I had reached the point of no return—when decisions were being made so fast, and there was no way back. I learned a whole new meaning of the psalm which says:

I lift up my eyes to the hills—where does my help come from? My help comes from the LORD, the Maker of heaven and earth.

Psalm 121:1–2 [NIV]

The idea that 'lifting up' and 'offering' might just be the same thing, led me, for the first time, to the principle that I should offer my eyes—the source of all my conflicts—to God; and that He would, somehow, be able to use them. In the end, this was the only thing left for me to do. God was teaching me to trust Him, the hard way. The place we had named the Well was a mess, too. Maris, one of the trustees, had chosen the name, as she wanted the place to be like the well at which Jesus sat and spoke to the woman who needed so badly to meet him. She came to the well to slake her thirst, but it was there that, as Jesus spoke to her, the wonderful offer of everlasting water was given by him—for all. Even with this encouraging truth in mind, it was difficult to view the state of the building with anything but astonishment. Yet hard work and prayer would eventually see our hopes fulfilled, as God blessed the work. We started with rotten floorboards, peeling paintwork; a broken window, and no telephone. There were no curtains at the windows, and the kitchen should have been put out of bounds, on health grounds. The lavatories were old, cracked and rusty. If the building looked like anything at all, in those early days, it certainly did not look like a peaceful place of healing!

All the money we had was given to solicitors to clear the legalities out of the way. If the building was to be made habitable, then the work would have to be done by us. There were days and days of hard work ahead. We were dirty, and broke!

"Oh Lord," I prayed, while digging out a floorboard, which dry rot had almost disintegrated, "we came here to work with you, not to scrub floors and paintwork! What will we do after all this hard work, if no-one comes near the place?"

The essential renovation and repairs were finally completed. Happily, our plans for the various rooms came to fruition. What started as an office has since been re-born, and is now a second private room. All the leaky holes in the roof were patched up, and the crumbling rain-drenched ceiling plaster renewed. The generosity of those who come to us now enables upkeep of the building to be carried out by professionals, instead of our willing, sore and amateurish hands.

12

CLEARING VISION

There are times when God's encouragement for the work that any of us are engaged in seems to descend on us by the bucketful.... A whole dollop was on its way, just when it was badly needed.

Sitting at home one evening, shortly after the opening of the Well, the phone rang. It was a friend, from the West Country, who had not been in touch for some months. After the pleasantries, she said, "Mike, I'm not sure what's happening to you these days, but I have a bit of Scripture for you. May I read it over the phone?" It was from Isaiah, and it was just for me:

And if you spend yourselves on behalf of the hungry and satisfy the needs of the oppressed, then your light will rise in the darkness, and your night will become like the noonday. The LORD will guide you always; he will satisfy your needs in a sun-scorched land and will strengthen your frame. You will be like a well-watered garden, like a spring whose waters never fail. Your people will rebuild the ancient ruins and will raise up the age-old foundations; you will be called Repairer of Broken Walls, Restorer of Streets with Dwellings.

Isaiah 58:9–12 [NIV]

God was listening to my every thought, and accepting my

every offering. He was going to change us—or at least me, as the scripture was for me—from a place of struggling disability, into a 'well-watered garden', which I later understood to be the Well. What was more, my 'night', by which I assumed He meant my lack of vision, was to be made into a noonday, through what was going on. Amazing! I was over the moon! For the time being He was not going to bring light to my eyes through all this; He was going to bring light to others. And the lovely folk who had opened the Centre with me—Ann, Maris, Sheila and Jean, who had joined us the year before, would become known as rebuilders and restorers. That is healing and wholeness! The whole Well Centre plan was going to work!

"Now," my caller went on, before I had time to relate the story of the opening of the Well. "Here is something else for you, as well. I don't know, but I think the Lord really wants you to have this gift— for yourself, and for you alone." She read from Proverbs, that a generous man would prosper, and that he who refreshes others will himself be refreshed. That was the moment when all the private financial worries flew out of the window, snuffed out by the sheer power of the Word of God. Not just them: all the hesitations over the money supply, to feed the Centre, vanished in the same breath.

More importantly—much more importantly—the people began to come. At first, they came in very small numbers, but the flow gradually increased, and there seemed no end to God's favour towards them. As people began to respond, I was reminded of the wonderful invitation:

Whoever is thirsty, let him come; and whoever wishes, let him take the free gift of the water of life.

Revelation 22:17 [NIV].

There were many miracles to watch, and much to give thanks for. It was not that we saw hundreds of people getting up out of wheelchairs, or throwing off medically incurable diseases; we saw our share of such things, but the real miracles came in the strengthening, the rebuilding, the refurbishing, the mending of broken lives to make whole people again—or as whole as we can be in a fallen world.

Although our eyes had been opened wide by all the teachings we had received over the years, it was God's grace which made things happen. Solicitors, doctors and drug addicts, airline pilots and single mothers, clergy and housewives; God does not mind who they are, or where they come from. And what were they bringing with them? Just about anything that it is possible to imagine: from abuse to M.E.; from sexual difficulties of all kinds to physical ailments; from mental illness to marriage strains. God touches all.

The Church's ministry of healing and wholeness is not necessarily about making people get better, but about bringing the peace, and knowledge of self-worth, which comes from reconciling yet more of our personhoods to God. In this way, everyone receives a measure of healing, and the thrill is electrifying.

During those early months, I was to take two severe knocks which, though shattering at the time, have worked to mend my own understanding of the apparently crazy question: 'How did a blind man finish up running a healing centre?' The first of these occurred in a tiny local church, to which I was invited to speak at a Ladies' Afternoon. I went along, very excited by the challenge, as here was a real opportunity to spread the gospel: that we did, indeed, have a loving God, who longs to satisfy the needs of His children, in whatever ways He would think best. It is a thrilling message, and thrilling to give.

At the end of the talk, after a formal vote of thanks, and a donation to the cause, one of the ladies came to thank me personally. She spoke quietly, and with great grace, but there was a sting in the tail.

"I might just have believed one tiny thing of what you said, if God healed you", she said. This was one of those awful moments, when the mind goes blank; and one knows full well what to say, about half an hour later! I should have told her that the Cross is the central symbol of the Christian faith, and I should have told her that the Cross is a symbol of suffering: that suffering and love and Christianity go together. I should have added that the principle of 'My

Life for Yours' is the central theme of Christianity, and that I was actually sharing in Jesus' suffering for the world—but I did not. I just went home feeling that I had probably let God down again, forgetting that He is far bigger than me!

That evening, it was reported to me that a close member of my family had decided that God was no good and that he would have nothing to do with the Church's idea that He was anything different. His justification was: "If God was any good, He would have healed Mike by now"! It was time to think; time to think out, quite clearly, how I could possibly justify, in my own mind, let alone anyone else's, what on earth I was doing leading a prayer community which was centred on Jesus and his healing hands. I would be asked the same questions, again and again. I wanted to be absolutely sure. Not just that, but if I could work out this paradox, then it might be encouraging to others in a similar situation, who wonder what they might do for God, when they themselves are less than whole in some way.

Two days later, I wrote these lines:

BROKEN TOGETHER

The gates of heaven came drifting wide
The day my Saviour hurt and died.
The body of Jesus, crucified.
What joy! What victory through pain!
What love released through the Lamb so slain!
What rapture, to exchange my loss
For a living share in heaven's Cross.
What honour, Lord, to share with thee
The sufferings of Calvary.
There is no place I'd rather be
Than standing, wounded, alongside thee.

The truth was steadily dawning. Disability affects the way that we relate to the world; it does not prevent us from having the relationship with God that He intends for us. Not just that, but, if our problems are offered up to Him, who is God Almighty, He is then free to use them, in His master plan to save the world. My own disability was fading into a background of blurred and distant unimportance. Anyway, life had become a tumbling rush, and there was much to do.

The earliest days at the Well were mad days of flying about between superstores, to buy paint and screws, and all the other things that are so essential in the setting up of a healing centre. Curtains, carpets, furniture, telephones and paint rollers—all these things filled our minds, from breakfast to teatime.

Grateful for the busyness, it was only at home that I came to grips with the not inconsiderable culture shock of going 'full time' for the Lord. In the ridiculously short space of two weeks, I had gone from being a heavy weight on myself, and all around me, to being the leader of a prayer community. Under the noise of banging hammers and steaming kettles, laughter at dirty faces and the joy of helping spouses, rumbled the old comments, tempting me to feel insecure in my new role.

"Physician, heal thyself!"

"I might believe it, if he sorted your eyes out for you."

"How can you say that God is good when He leaves you like this?"

As if my now battered soul were not succeeding quite well enough in squeezing out any confidence I might have started with, Satan was about to join in.

"What sort of an example are you?"

"People will think you're talking through the top of your head."

"If He won't heal you, why should He help anyone else?"

"Nobody will come to the Well, because they'll see you and know that it doesn't work."

This, I now believe, was God's reassuring reply: I had been reading about Samuel, as he had been sorting through seven brothers, attempting to find the one whom God wanted him to anoint as king of Israel. God had said these words to him, somewhere down the selection process, but they were also to be the complete answer to my internal criticism:

The LORD does not look at the things man looks at. Man looks at the outward appearance, but the LORD looks at the heart.

I Samuel 16:7 [NIV]

If I were to lead a team of people, whose great desire was to be healing channels of God's grace, then it would have to be my heart that got cleaned up, rather than my blindness which needed to be corrected. I did not need new eyes as much as I needed a new heart. First, in the light of my own experiences, I felt the need to understand better the whole subject of suffering. If we were going to minister to it, we had better see clearly the field we were to plough. It seems that suffering, at any level, from the shallowest to the deepest, is a series of threads that run through each and every one of our lives. It may seem strange, at first sight, that the opposite of suffering is not the total lack of it, but peace in it, or at least through it; and the key to this peace is acceptance. This 'acceptance' is not the surrender of our situation to 'fate', with statements such as, 'We all have our own problems', or, 'I just have to live with it!' Those are submissions to 'fate'. They admit what is a great untruth: that we are at the mercy of our problems.

The central issue of suffering, in Christianity, is the Cross of Jesus—at one and the same time the best and the worst thing that has ever happened in the world.

'Here is love', says the scripture, 'not that we loved God, but that He loved us and gave Himself.' This love is not a mood or a feeling, nor a sentiment, but an act of will; His love wills only the very best for us—our joy, and our peace. I have met so many Christians with real problems, turning their lives over to the will of God; after all, we have no idea what He will do with them; no view of the problems in store, and no sense of balance about what might be lost in the process.

After about two years of finding our feet together in marriage, Ginnie and I had decided to have children, to complete the family. All our thoughts about this decision, which led to the arrival of James and Robert, were concentrated around the reasons why, but in the end we knew that we just wanted them. In that sense, the decision was non-rational: just a step towards fulfilment of life. But, then, any parent knows that having and bringing up children is a sacrifice. In the process of planning a family, parents have little regard for the problems which may, or may not, come later. It is an act of total commitment; a sacrifice of love, without the cost being counted in advance. A parent knows what it means to say, 'My life for yours', which is the whole principle of the Cross and the Christian faith.

Surely, this is exactly what faith is all about. If we truly believe that someone loves us, then we trust them. The will of God and the love of God are the same thing, and love suffers. If I were to condense my emerging theology about the love of God into a nutshell, I would say that the only way I have of knowing about this love is to know that He gave up His majesty to become a man, and that Jesus gave up his life for me. Love is bound up in sacrifice.

Sitting down and thinking about it, I found that many of these beliefs were not based on the use of brain power, or rationality. I was just accepting them as part of the mystery of God: the virgin birth, the holy trinity, the transfiguration, resurrection. No-one had ever properly explained the holy trinity to me—I just accept it. These things are all mysteries. Suffering in the world, alongside a loving and caring God, is just one such mystery; and we cannot explain that one, either!

God so needs to remind us, for our sakes, not of who we are but of who He is. In tracing the Bible story of Job, a book every sufferer should read, we noticed that he reached his point of utter desolation. I suppose poor Job had lost much more than I had, but the feelings were much the same. When he lost everything, still believing that good people like himself ought not to fall foul of such upsets, he prayed:

Will you never look away from me, or let me alone even for an instant? If I have sinned, what have I done to you, O watcher of men? Why have you made me your target? Have I become a burden to you?
Job 7:19–20 [NIV]

When Job screamed out his pain at God, not doubting for one moment that God is there, and in control, he was just so angry that God was allowing such awful things to happen to him. He hurled all those questions at God, just like me; and when God finally broke His silence, it was not with any answers. Instead, He showered Job with more questions. God did not give Job a single answer—just as He has not answered me. His only response to Job was the mystery of Himself.

Where were you when I laid the earth's foundation? Tell me, if you understand. Who marked off its dimensions? Surely you know! Who stretched a measuring line across it? On what were its footings set, or who laid its cornerstone—while the morning stars sang together and all the angels shouted for joy?

Who shut up the sea behind doors when it burst forth from the womb, when I made the clouds its garment and wrapped it in thick darkness, when I fixed limits for it and set its doors and bars in place, when I said, 'This far you may come and no farther; here is where your proud waves halt'?

Have you ever given orders to the morning, or shown the dawn its place, that it might take the earth by the edges and shake the wicked out of it?

Have you journeyed to the springs of the sea or walked in the recesses of the deep? Have the gates of death been shown to you? Have you seen the gates of the shadow of death? Have you comprehended the vast expanses of the earth? Tell me, if you know all this.

What is the way to the abode of light? And where does darkness reside? Can you take them to their places? Do you know the paths to their dwellings? Surely you know, for you were already born! You have lived so many years!

Do you send the lightning bolts on their way? Do they report to you, 'Here we are'? Who endowed the heart with wisdom or gave understanding to the mind? Who has the wisdom to count the clouds? Who can tip over the water jars of the heavens when the dust becomes hard and the clods of earth stick together?

Do you hunt the prey for the lioness and satisfy the hunger of the lions when they crouch in their dens or lie in wait in a thicket? Who provides food for the raven when its young cry out to God and wander about for lack of food?

Job 38:4–13, 16–21, 35– 41 [NIV]

Question after question; but God is revealing something to Job about who He really is. In earlier years I might have dismissed these words of God as plainly unscientific and therefore untrue, but science is only God's way of gently releasing to His people the knowledge of how it all works. If we knew it all, there would be no such thing as mystery, research and discovery. These questions are not the results of a science exam, but a statement of majesty. God had done the same to Job as He did to me when I first read the story; He was using the fact that Job was on his back to make him look up, to behold the majesty of His greatness.

In the course of my ministry, since those far off teenage days on the river bank down in Hampshire, it has been my joy to pray with (among many others) a number of sufferers from M.E., that most debilitating of illnesses. During a long period of bedridden collapse, one sufferer had found more than enough time to indulge in some serious contemplation of her future. She was totally dependent on her family for everyday care. This lady was blessed with a husband and children who were particularly loving, and tolerant of the destruction that M.E. so readily causes to home life. During this enforced period of suffering, she realized that her life might go on for a very long time, past the day when her children grew up and left home. Even her dear husband could not be completely relied on, since all mortal men become ill sometimes and do (may heaven forbid) get run over by buses! It was in that moment that she knew, for the first time, her utter dependence on God; and the truth that Jesus was the only person on whom she could entirely rely. This was to be the day that her healing began to flow.

Neither Job on his ash heap, nor I on my river bank, nor the lady healed of M.E., have ever denied God's existence. Again, we remember that even the question, 'why me?' presupposes that there is a Deity: a Being with a plan or purpose. We did not imagine that God had nothing to do with our troubles, but we had a thousand questions.

Sitting on that winding Hampshire bank-side, so long ago, I could not have known that years later, deeply involved in the Church's ministry of healing and wholeness, I would still be asking the same sort of questions. Somehow—in all the answered prayers, and in all the thrills and joys of lives made new—God, in His wisdom, has not seen fit to heal me of my own disease. I was blinder than ever. I yelled at God: "What is wrong with me? Why am I still having to wait, or is there still something you find so distasteful that you can't be merciful to me? I know you have the power and the authority; but where is the will? Is there some reason you have, for not healing me? Is there something in my make-up, which stops me from receiving your healing?"

Each time I have seen His hand working in healing ways in other people, I feel—albeit, sometimes, ever so slightly—a fresh hammer blow to my imagined unworthiness. As the years go by, though, God is seeing to it that this pain diminishes, and today it is all too easily swamped by the excitements of His whole-making love, pouring into others through prayer, and through the ministry of the Church.

God is God: three mighty Persons in one; and He loves us. We are not adrift in a sea of chaos. In the moments when my mood is down, when I fail to be full of praise and thanksgiving, I only find peace again by returning to the One who is unchanging: the God who wants to be alongside; the God who wants to be there with us—the Rock; the Refuge. We are held in the everlasting arms, and we can therefore be at peace. This is faith; this is trust. I may not like what happens; I may even hate it sometimes, but I have still learned to trust Him. If I really do want to be a disciple, then I must take up my cross, and follow. Jesus is the same Lord: yesterday, before all this happened to me; today, as I go blind; and tomorrow—when who knows what will be happening.

I found these words, which caught my frame of mind:

Because the Sovereign LORD helps me, I will not be disgraced. Therefore have I set my face like flint, and I know I will not be put to shame.

Isaiah 50:7 [NIV]

Once again, I found myself offering my sight to the Lord. This is an act of submission which has now become a regular event in my daily prayer, along with all the complicated accompanying emotions. I say something like this:

"Well, Lord, you have promised to help me but you have a funny way of doing it! All the hundreds of hours of prayer that must have gone into this situation, and still I'm not restored! Why won't you do what I want you to do?"

The answer is always the same: "Trust me. I know what I am doing."

I was beginning to accept His will; to accept that for me, at this point in my life, the blindness was part of being with Him. What He could make of it all was His business—and not mine to question. Here, I glimpsed the long-avoided truth; the sound of the awful word I never wanted to hear. That word was 'acceptance'. It was time to think about accepting what had happened to me.

13

LEARNING TO THANK

Our saying to anyone who comes to the Well, "Accept this suffering", does not sound at all reasonable; but, then, there has never been any inclination to do that. God sends people to the Well whom He wants to help. Far be it from us to do anything but just be alongside them in the healing Light which is Jesus Christ.

Even so, many in the modern Church, even some of those working within the healing ministry, would find such a remark little short of repugnant. To accept suffering is quite contrary to human nature and, of course, it cannot be right to accept everything as if there is nothing that can be done. There are things which can and should be changed. There are things that can be changed and should not be; but 'acceptance' is the thing we need for those matters we would like to change, but cannot.

St. Paul prayed three times for the removal of the thorn from his flesh, and the only answer given was that God's grace was to be sufficient. In other words, God said 'no'. As we noted earlier, he said that he was 'given' a thorn in his flesh, to prevent him from being big-headed over some spiritual experience which had happened to him earlier.

When we read of Paul asking no fewer than three times for the removal of the thorn, and we read of Jesus asking the Father if it would be possible to remove from him the cup from which he would have to drink, then we know that there is absolutely nothing wrong with asking God to heal our diseases or our relationship difficulties, or to sort out our finances—even though we may be where we are because we are where He wants us to be!

Since I have come to accept that God is God, and that He allows blindness to continue for His purposes; and that, therefore, I am part of His purposes, I have still often ended a time of prayer by saying: "Anytime you're ready, Lord, I'm still waiting to have my sight back." I am not praying against His will by saying such things; but, when the answer is 'no', I can only accept it, knowing that He has something much better in store for me. Greater things are at stake, in the invisible Kingdom to which we belong, and towards which we grow. Psalm 116 asks how we might possibly repay the Lord for all His goodness to us, and we have so much to thank God for. There are so many good things in our lives, despite all our sorrows. Even those who have nothing have the gift of life itself.

God may not have healed me yet, but He gave me my wildest dreams! Early retirement was one of these dreams, and God has given it to me at the age of forty eight! Having the time to lean on gateposts and watch the world go by, while meditating on the more important things of life, was a schoolboy ambition I had thrown out years ago, thinking it was born out of laziness. But here it was.

Having a boss, namely Himself, who would actually be pleased to see me in the mornings, would be another dream come true! Sufficient income, on which to live without struggling, had been organised; and, gift of all gifts, there was the Well Centre. For three years, our hearts had longed for a place of quiet peace and prayer; a refuge for those who need God; a place to receive His healing love— and here we were. A psalm echoes my prayers:

LORD, you have assigned me my portion and my cup; you have made my lot secure. The boundary lines have fallen for me in pleasant places; surely I have a delightful inheritance.

Psalm 16:5 [NIV]

In His grace, I was pushed—not entirely unwillingly—into a place of leadership for the community, which did not sit too easily, even after a working lifetime in management. 'I am not', I repeatedly reminded myself, 'the right man for the job. After all, how can I organise appointments without reading a diary? How can I talk to lots of people on the phone if I cannot see the telephone directory, and—most worryingly of all—how would I preach, or give lectures, without sheaves of notes?'

My worries about coping with all these questions have been melted away by the team effort of the community, and the biggest one—drying up when giving a talk without notes—has simply not materialized. I have actually found it a huge advantage to see only the front row, and then only vaguely. The nerves become less frayed at the edges, when there only seem to be a few folk listening; a great help in the early days of speaking!

In Psalm 116, the writer confesses that he does not know how to express his gratitude to the provider of all things, in a way that would be pleasing and acceptable to Him. It would be good to find the right gift, to give to express my thankfulness. As I thought about this, it occurred to me that the best presents for those whom we love are not the quick-fix book tokens that get sucked off the shop display stands by an over-hurried giver, but rather the personal things, which have been carefully chosen. These are the ones which get the best reception, and give the greatest joy. So what could I possibly do for God, who was delivering me from my troubles? He had brought me up out of slavery—better known as working in a factory—and He had freed me from all future concerns, by having me work with Him, instead. He had surrounded me with Christians, whose only desire was—and still is—to love God more tomorrow than they did yesterday, in the full knowledge that this deepening relationship would become a healing force in the world.

What could I give to God, who had given me everything? The psalmist says:

I will take up the cup of salvation and call on the name of the LORD

Psalm 116:13

Here, I found my answer. The greatest thanksgiving gift I could give God would be to take the cup of salvation. But what was in it? Whatever may be in my cup—the rejections and the sorrows, the losses and the joys—I would be ready and willing to take it, because I trust Him. I can also now pray: 'Lord, I need your thunder sometimes, because your music alone doesn't serve me. I need emotional pain sometimes, not too much and not too often; but, if I am to be reforged for you—a daily rather than a one-off process—remoulded, to fit some unseen plan in which I trust, then I need a degree of suffering to shape me, as well as the joy.'

Perhaps suffering is an integral part of my discipleship; a vital part of my relationship with God. By now, it was really coming home to me that salvation is a cup, not only containing our high times and joys but everything that is necessary for our redemption—offered by a loving God, who wants only the best for us. It contains only those things that are needed for the redemption of ourselves and for the world, through Jesus Christ. This walk of discipleship is a gift from God.

Anyone who receives presents from friends and family, at anniversary times, knows that the natural response is to say 'thank you'. Not everything which is given to us fills us with excitement, nor may it answer a long-standing prayer, but we still summon up sufficient grace to thank the giver for thinking of us. Some of the things I find in my own particular 'cup' of discipleship do not appeal at all, but I still try to honour the Giver by thanking Him. Not easy! The honouring comes as I give the giver the credit—just as it would be with earthly gifts. No-one looks at the label on a Christmas present, and says to himself, 'This is a gift from Birmingham, or Stoke-on-Trent, or from Tokyo'; we say that this is a gift from a person: the giver.

Until that eventful Christmas, when the Spirit of God hugged me at the altar rail, I claimed that all that I had was a result of my own endeavours, hard application and the successful conquest of my disability—my own fight, in a sighted world. I know now that this is not reality. I got the source wrong. The strength for that fight had come from God. As far as I can remember, it has always been easy to give thanks when things are going well—when family life seems well-ordered and there is money in the bank. But what about those times when we feel kicked around by people, or organisations, or events; and when life is caving in on us? Could it be that the Lord is allowing us to go through times of testing, as James says, "for the maturing of our faith"? Giving thanks becomes very much more difficult when the golf ball has gone into the rough. Proverbs 3:6 says to us, "In all your ways acknowledge Him, and He will make your paths straight." [NIV.] I can receive everything that is in the 'cup' of discipleship which is offered to me, as a whole, including the things which may entail suffering for the Kingdom's sake. I can give thanks for the cup, because it has been given, by Almighty God, as part of His great purpose of salvation.

In this context, it would seem such a small thing, in eternal terms, that God should have noticed the Moabite widow—who was suffering loneliness and poverty, as she worked in the fields outside Bethlehem—and made it possible for her to meet Boaz. This is the sort of thing that happens a thousand times a day, around the world, without even a single thought towards the author of the event. Out of the union of Ruth and Boaz came baby Obed; and from him came Jesse, then David, and on to Jesus.

His purposes are being worked out in many things which happen, whether or not we feel comfortable with our part in His plan. When we give thanks to God in all circumstances, we do Him honour, and give Him credit for who and what He is. Psalm 50:23 is a reminder that it is when we sacrifice thank-offerings that we honour God; and, in doing so, we prepare the way—so that God may show us His salvation planning.

It took a long time to dawn on me, but I eventually began to see that this scripture is vibrantly true. I began to learn to thank Him for the whole of life, both whilst going through those things which were hard to bear, and the obviously good things. I began to see benefits — not for myself, but for Him and for others. Losing my eyes played a major role in seeing me removed from secular employment and dumped, rather unceremoniously, into the Church's healing ministry. I am where He wants me to fit into His plan, and going blind has played an intricate part in ensuring that I got there.

How can I do anything but have peace in accepting His plan, albeit I really do not understand it; and how can I have anything but joy in the certain knowledge of being part of that plan?

Shortly after the Well opened, we met a mother whose son had fallen victim as a baby to cerebral palsy, which resulted in his having the body of a twelve year old and the mind of a newborn child. Being a believing Christian, she hauled her little son all over the country, visiting anyone who had any sort of reputation in the Church for a healing ministry. Her agonised search for his healing was made even more difficult by Christian friends, who told her that she was exhibiting lack of faith by continuously searching in this way. God had heard her prayers, she was told, and all she had to do now was to exercise faith, and wait for His blessing to arrive.

Despite this somewhat dubious advice, she continued with their trek, until her son died. I wanted so much to tell her that it was fine to go on crying out to God, and that she should also be giving thanks that He was in control of the family situation. But, at these times, such words are hard to come by. I met her again, after her son had died, and she was able to say how much she now thanked God for his life, and for all that the experience had taught her. I felt very small.

Spending a long weekend with Bishop Ban It Chiu, during that first summer at the Well, I plucked up the courage to ask him to pray with me once again, about my own suffering. I use the words 'pluck up courage' not from excessive awe of the man, even given his great spiritual stature, but against the possibility of being disappointed, yet again, by seemingly unanswered prayer. He surprised me somewhat, by replying, "He who shall be first shall be last." I waited all day with growing anticipation, knowing that God sometimes leaves the best gifts until last. Perhaps, now, I was about to receive what would be a wonderful boost to life. Eventually, at the end of the day, we met for prayer. Towards the end of that time, the dear Bishop said to me, "The trouble is, Mike, the Lord says that your blindness is the only thing that keeps you totally dependent on Him. Your blindness keeps you in obedience." Within a few moments, he followed up this one crashing blow as he confirmed his earlier word for me: "The Lord doesn't have enough disabled people in the healing ministry." This was not coming any easier the second time round!

I felt much as those four friends must have done, as they lowered the paralysed man down through the roof to Jesus' feet, only to hear him say, "Your sins are forgiven." My first reaction was to say,

"Well, thanks, Lord; thanks a bunch. That's not what I wanted to hear at all!"

I wanted healing, and I was not going to get it at this time. Whoever I prayed with, however much they longed to have me see again, the disappointment came rushing back. There were so many Christians promising the healing power of God to those who asked. I longed for it with all my heart. I went off to be alone, and complained, cried and yelled at God. But, then, I was reminded that it was the sacrifice of thanksgiving which honours Him. I began to do just this—to offer that sacrifice of praise and thanksgiving, in my heart.

Nothing had changed: God was still God, and still in charge. I was not adrift in a sea of chaos. The sun had been shining in the heavens before my appointed time with the Bishop, and it was still shining now. The birdsong, which lifted my heart as I had gone into that meeting, was still there to welcome me back. God was before, and God is after. God has a plan for me, which necessitates His keeping me very close, and dependent on Him. Whatever that plan is, the best is yet to come. One obvious outworking of this 'keeping close' idea was the fact that failing sight had doubtless been the major chemical in the formula which had removed me from the factory. If my sight had been healed, I would surely still be there, in secular employment; and God would not have been able to display such great grace towards me in some very specific ways.

Psalm 50:23 tells me that thanksgiving prepares the way, so that God may show me His salvation. The question which ran through my mind on the river bank, at the age of nineteen, still lived with me. So, what will happen tomorrow? The sheer thrill of knowing that God has a plan which personally involves me, and that I might glimpse some of that in the days and years to come, gently began to swallow down all my disappointment. The tears dried away in the sunshine. In the space of half an hour, I made the spiritual journey from being on my knees, and beaten, to being three feet above the ground.

So I began to see the nature of the relationship with God which He requires of me in these things. I take the cup of salvation, which contains all those things I need, whether I agree or not. I say, "Thank you, Lord," because in doing so I honour Him, by crediting Him with being the author of my salvation. I offer myself, my life—all that I am—back to Him, I trust as an act of pure obedience, along with many of the attendant emotions that spring to mind.

What will happen, then, to all I am—the real me—which is released back to God? The answer is 'transformation'. God takes that gift, and His love transforms it into something He can use—as He used the broken body and shed blood of Jesus to give life to the world (and shows us this in broken bread and poured out wine). The ingredient which causes that transformation to occur is God's love. One most lovely example of this was the sight of a six year old girl rushing into the kitchen, clutching a broken daffodil in her sweaty hand, and holding it up to her mother as a gift of adoration. The reactions of the mother were conclusive proof that love transforms everything. The look on her face might have been described as divine. If all I have to offer God is a broken daffodil, eyes that do not work too well, my frustrations when I fail to do something I ought to be able to do, God does not despise that gift. His love transforms it into something wonderful. I found this little piece, tucked away in a psalm:

The sacrifices of God are a broken spirit; a broken and contrite heart, O God, you will not despise.

Psalm 51:17 [NIV]

I do not suppose that little girl understood the warm glow in her mother's heart, though she would never have doubted its coming, nor that love would transform some apparently useless object into a thing of great beauty in the eyes of the receiver, but that does not matter. What the mother received is of far higher value than the gift itself, and the little girl began to know the warmth of giving, and the receiving back that comes from it. Whatever form the flower takes, God, in His grace, says, "thank you". When His love has changed the gift into something else, it is handed back to us, perhaps in a very different form, for us to receive, give thanks for, and offer back again.

Realising and experiencing such transforming grace has underlined, for me, that surrender is a vital part of ministering and teaching about divine healing. It is an uphill struggle on occasions, as all most of us want is to get better—rather than to deepen our relationship with God, and find wholeness along that road.

We have found that if we give Him all that we are (whether or not we are suffering from some disease or disability) He will give us renewal, refreshment, and His living water, in our hearts. In exchange for our sufferings, He gives us His joys; for our battles He gives us His peace; for our wildernesses He gives us His pastures to graze in. This is the fundamental principle of the Cross: my sins for His righteousness; my deaths for His life. Everything is material for sacrifice; for offering back, for God to use. Every loss has its pains, every up has its down, and there is always sunshine after rain.

I have never been able to say that one gift to me has been the result of any particular 'offering prayer', but one enormous encouragement comes to mind. Hilary Kent, from the Harnhill Centre, once introduced me to a group of guests, at the start of a ministry week in Gloucestershire, by saying, "This is Mike, who doesn't see very well—but don't worry about it; he can see with his ears more than most of us can hear with our eyes!" And don't we all need people like her, to confirm us in our vocation! I took her words as a great compliment, but give thanks to God for replacing my brokenness with something far more useful to Himself.

To apply 2 Timothy 1:8, I would say that I will not be ashamed to testify about our Lord, nor ashamed of myself even as I inhabit the prison of disability, as long as I am living in His will. It is in that will alone that I find true peace and joy. So I will join with all the saints down the ages who suffer for the gospel, by the power of God.

14

THE THORN TREE

It did not take long for the next truth to fall into the hearts of the good folk who opened the healing centre, and into mine, too. Perhaps, if the hurting folk we wanted to help could see the love of Christ when they walked into the Well, and not imagine some blind guy trying to be something he was not, then God's purposes would be well served. God had not yet healed me in one particular way, but a heart transparent to His love would surely be of more use to Him.

I had been gently encouraged by Harnhill to seek this as the true nature of healing and wholeness. Cleaning out any wrong thing would mean more of the good: more of me to love God with; and, as a direct consequence, more from God to love others with. This 'cleaning' ministry is not just to help us to love God more, but also so that those we touch can be better fed through His healing grace. As a leading Christian psychiatrist once expressed, to a group of eager students: "How dare you operate on other people, without having first washed your own hands!"

The concept of loving God more fully tomorrow than was possible yesterday is not such a strange one, when compared with the feelings that two people have for each other in the latter years of a successful marriage.

The bright-eyed bride on her wedding day might be hard pushed to imagine that she might ever love her husband more than she did at that moment in time but, if only it were possible to take snapshots of feelings before and after some process of change, she might be truly amazed to see the difference in their relationship after many years of a happy marriage.

In the same way, it is so difficult to explain to anyone who has a relationship with God that, if it is worked on and allowed to flourish and grow, it can, in the course of time, become a thing of great beauty, and a joy in the heart. The by-product of such a relationship, when it is growing, becomes obvious: we love others more and more. We were slowly discovering this truth, not through any effort on our own part, but through the simple effect of becoming more transparent to the burning love of God Himself, who dwells within us.

No wonder Jesus gave a double answer to a single question, when asked which he thought was the greatest commandment. He was asked which commandment in the law was to be considered as the greatest. His answer was that we should love the Lord our God with all our heart, and with all our soul, and with all our mind. This, he said, is to be thought of as the greatest, and first, commandment. And a second commandment is like it. We should love our neighbour as we might ourselves. To love God, and to love our neighbour, are two distinct commands, but are inseparable. The one follows on quite naturally of its own accord behind the other. We were discovering for ourselves that the first one is prior. We love God more tomorrow than we did yesterday by having more of our inner bits surrendered to Him. In this way, there is more of us to love Him with, and His love then flows more freely through us, into those whom we encounter along the way.

This was how I wanted to grow: I wanted an increase in that transparency. These might be high ideals, but this is a key ingredient of what is sometimes called the ministry of reconciliation. 'Mind you,' I reminded myself, as I reflected on these things, 'I could do with having my sight back as well!'

Shortly after the Well opened, I was given an introduction to the Reverend Fred Pritchard. At that time, before his retirement, he was a national board member of the Wholeness Through Christ movement

(WTC). What was more, the dear man lived only about five miles away! "Fred," I told him, "I don't want to be an unguided missile. I need some sort of framework around us, which allows us to do whatever we feel is right, but as we get near the wall of the frame we need to know that we are probably out of order." Freedom to minister in the Spirit, within a framework—that was what we wanted; and not just any old framework. We needed one that was acceptable to the Church: one which was Bible-based, and which enjoyed godly and recognised oversight; full of love and compassion; and, most of all, full of healing and wholeness of life with God.

We longed for a framework in which we could help others; not just to get from God whatever was going, but to enter into the fullness of resurrection life. If, in the process of finding such a framework, the Church could minister to me, and get rid of anything they came across which might be hindering the free flow of my love to God—and therefore the equally free flow of His Holy Spirit into needy people— then what a super added bonus that would be! WTC seemed to have the exact ingredients we were searching for. They had a ministry framework; they had great teachers; they would teach us to minister, and they would minister to us.

This was to be a three-year course, with practical ministry in between. Problems loomed, as soon as it became evident that travelling, and being in strange places away from home, would be necessary. Rushing ahead, on a wave of spiritual enthusiasm, is wonderful fun; but, yet again, I had got myself totally committed to something, without a second thought for practicalities. How was I going to manage train stations and timetables, find taxis at the other end, learn the geography and, and, and...?

As God would have it, Jean Hadfield, by now a well-established minister in the group, had also committed herself to the WTC 'treadmill', so I had my first 'guide dog'! The third and final course in the WTC trilogy of week-long conferences was held in a beautiful and historic retreat house, on the outskirts of a village in the heart of Lancashire. Three particular visions of delight spring back to mind from those days, far from home. The first concerned food—such an important subject for any man away from home! The second was one of those lovely senses that rise up somehow from the feet, to fill the whole body. I was so near to the county of my adopted roots. Walking around the village, hanging onto the elbow of the long-suffering Jean Hadfield from the Well, I stomped along cobbled lanes, and leaned on drystone walls and black stone river bridges.

As we walked along the pavements, I could run my free hand along the old, black wrought iron railings which edged the elevated pavements at the front of the dark stone cottages—with their brilliant white paintwork, and the black and white contrast between stone block walls and pointing. The atmosphere flooded my soul, like ice cream in a dry mouth on a hot day. Just across the border, where the same cobbles, steep hills and stone walls abound, was the countryside which had been the adopted 'flower bed' for my roots.

"Just over there, somewhere, is Yorkshire," I told Jean, "but I don't expect a mere southerner to appreciate that!" Yorkshire was my first real job. Yorkshire was industry and history; but, more than anything, Yorkshire was Ginnie. I could feel the presence of the place, oozing over the top of the distant hills, carried over to me on the gentle easterly breeze.

"Why can't I work in the North, Lord? I would find it much more fun!" There was no reply. "You see, Jean," I remember adding by way of trying to explain the feeling, "God created Yorkshire, and then He just hung the rest of the world around the outside of it!" She smiled, ignoring the comment. There was more—much more—to come.

The third experience was a true gift to me from the Lord; something to hang on to, and to use whenever I needed to. It was a full-size cinemascope, multi coloured, panoramic, moving three-dimensional picture, which is only too easy to recall at will, and is frequently revisited, when I need reminding how and why I finished up in places that can be so exhilarating and so exhausting—so anxious for God to work, and so 'gobsmacked' when He did! This, frankly, was awesome. What was to come was a true gift from a very loving Father; something I could invest in, some real piece of security, something that could be used again and again, whenever the time would be right; in other words, the perfect gift. At the start of a three-hour time of prayerful ministry, with two of the course leaders, I had said to them, "Whatever happens this afternoon, please don't get into praying about my eyesight. I've been messed around too much by people just wanting to have a go; this thing is now an integral part of my relationship with God, and all the prayer in the world won't shift it now."

This must have seemed terribly ungracious, and less than Christian, but, for as long as I can remember, opticians and doctors have asked to examine my eyes out of pure curiosity, rather than any ability to help. I am a human being, not a guinea pig. There have been Christians, too, who have seen me as a bit of a challenge and, with much love and respect for all of them, their approach does not always feel like love.

I think they were quite shocked by what they heard, and saw my bold statement as lack of faith, and disbelief, but the story seemed too long to bother them with. It would have taken the whole session, and more, to go through all the aching and struggling steps that had brought me to a place of peace in Christ without healing; and the time was not to be wasted in giving these dear ones a lecture in theology. Why should I ask for a stone, when God may be wanting to give me bread? I was sure that God had more important things to do in this time allotted for prayer ministry.

They asked me about stumbling blocks; about my emotions on going blind and—to my dismay, because I thought it was all over and done with—my working relationship with the Church hierarchy. Was I getting paranoid?

The talking went on and on. Eventually, the leaders began to ask God to express His feelings for me in some tangible way, to help me along the rough ways. I am sure I had not drifted off to sleep, but a dream of such reality followed, that I can only think that I may well have done!

There is a certain soporific combination of warm summer sunshine, one heavily rewarding lunch, and soft gentle prayer, that causes the best of us to do a little drifting. I saw myself walking barefoot, along a stony path, which lay across the face of a rolling, heather-strewn mountain. I could even hear a curlew call on the distant hillside, giving up a mournful cry which so well reflected the loneliness of my journey. The heather was in flower; the blueberries were bright blue, and the bees were busy with the clover. Not a single cloud whitened the deep blue above me, and a soft breeze was ruffling my hair. At right angles to my path lay another track, coming down from the hilltop to my left, towards the valley floor; and there, on his way down, came, slowly walking, the lonesome figure of Jesus.

His bare feet were cut to ribbons by the jagged edges of the ground beneath and, when I glanced down, so were mine. The soles were bruised and grazed, aching with tiredness, and the ankles were puffed up, like potatoes. Straightaway, we had something in common: feet which were cut and bruised from walking through the world.

'This is wonderful,' I thought. 'Here, at last, is someone to talk to, someone who would really understand; someone with all the time in the world to listen.' A nearby thorn tree, just below where the two paths met, cast a shadow large enough to sit under, and to provide shelter from the heat of the day. There he sat, beckoning for me to join him. There were no words that passed between us: I just sat beside him, a little to his right and a little behind, so that, beyond the back of his head, I could see what he was seeing. I remember being so thankful that bad eyesight never prevents people from looking with spiritual eyes, or feeling atmospheres with spiritual senses.

I wanted to comment on the fact that we shared bruised feet, in the hope that he might heal the soreness, but no words came. I wanted to ask him to touch my eyes with his finger, but suddenly it just did not seem important any more. Jesus seemed lost in his own thoughts; not concerned with my affairs, but with those of others in the valley villages below, and on the opposite hillsides. This was no time to talk.

My bleeding feet lay pointing up to the sky, about six inches from his right hand. He would only have to stretch a little forward, and my struggling walk through life would be so much easier. I willed and ached for him to do it, but he would not move. Then again, his feet were damaged, too, and I was not about to offer to heal them for him, either! Perhaps damaged feet were a gift to me, so that I could share just a little in his pain? When I began to see what he was looking at, I discovered with quite a shock that my feet, and their little difficulties, had gone out of focus. They did not seem important any more to me, either. As his gaze moved slowly back and forth along the line of blue and grey hills, my eyes followed the movement of his head, and all I could see was pain.

There were grieving widows, failing husbands and wounded children; and there were so many people whose illnesses were the real kings of their lives, ruling over everything and destroying the peace in their souls. There was anger and frustration, depression and unhappiness. There was anxiety and unfulfilment, and hearts with little vacuums in them, which longed to be filled with something permanent—but were searching, fruitlessly, for whatever might make life more bearable and take away the pain. I suppose there must have been happy people as well—it is just that I did not notice them. The broken ones were much easier to see, for some reason. They stood out from the crowd, and were in the majority. If I could have seen Jesus' face at that moment, I am sure I would have seen him crying. I looked, again, towards the valley towns, with the vision of an eagle, and saw the worst thing of all—mothers holding dead babies in their arms, so shocked in their own pain that they could not find the emotion to respond to the horror of their situations. Whether or not Jesus was crying, I will never know, but I did.

Such a sight of horror was too much to bear. These were the words that sprang to mind, as the centre of my concentration lifted from my aching feet to the aching world. The words were the sounds from the lips of those fathers and mothers and children below me, who had raised their faces towards our hillside position, and had caught sight of Jesus.

"I lift up my eyes to the hills—where does my help come from? My help comes from the LORD, the Maker of heaven and earth."

"Send me down to the valley, Lord," I said, "and let me help them." Whatever happened that day was yet to be revealed, but the meeting was closing with a warm glow. The Bible says:

A man of many companions may come to ruin, but there is a friend who sticks closer than a brother.

Proverbs 18:24 [NIV]

That was true! Then it was the end of my allotted time, and the end of the course. The next day would be the journey home to the valley country of Wales.

Into the Well they began to come—one after another, in a steady stream. Beautiful people who should be flowering for Christ, and yet were flattened by the aftermath of miscarriages, abortions, stillborn children, cot deaths and teenage suicide. Of course, there were still many others, with other sorts of dragchutes on their lives. God has been so gracious to all who have been willing to receive His love, but these ones from the vision were the ones to really steal my heart away. I lost sight of my own 'torn feet'. God was doing something for me by replacing my sorrows with the sorrows of others; my pain for me, with His pain for them. He was exchanging their hurts for His healing love; their deaths for His salvation; their sorrows for His joys, their griefs for His peace. His healing grace releases the screwed-down tension of the years, and what joy it is, through the misty eyes of Christ's tears, to watch the flowers of his Kingdom grow and blossom, to his glory.

It was some months after the Lancashire picture that I woke up one morning, shouting, "Eureka!" I had been dreaming of the shade and the rest underneath the thorn tree, during the night before, and had realised, yet again, God's faithfulness to me. I remembered sitting under the same tree, in prayer with Paul Mainwaring, nine years before! Then, I had prayed for another man to sit with in the shade, and now he had arrived. Since then, repeated trips have been made to the thorn tree and, each time, the feet are less bruised than before. The path is smoother. Two years earlier, the team at the Well had felt that we could not be overwhelmed by any force which was not of

God if, and only if, everything we did and said was done in love. This resolution was really beginning to pay off.

Once, we had been an object of suspicion. Now, a few clergy had begun to come to us. Pastors were recommending to their people that they should come to the Well, for prayer ministry.

We had begun to teach the deeper things of God more publicly, and greater numbers drifted in to the teaching days, which we started to hold at the Well. As our love for the Almighty grew, so did our love for others; and the grace of God seemed to inform and release our ministry, more and more.

The letter to the Hebrews says:

Therefore, strengthen your feeble arms and weak knees. "Make level paths for your feet," so that the lame may not be disabled, but rather healed. Make every effort to live in peace with all men and to be holy; without holiness, no-one will see the Lord.

Hebrews 12:13 [NIV]

'Make a level path for my feet'? — Where had that come up before? Did John the Baptist not say, "Make straight the way of the Lord"?

So this is the ministry of healing: to make the path of the Lord straight and level. This is peace: the knowledge that, whatever else is going on, we are tucked up safely in the everlasting arms, and can say: 'All things come of thee, and of thine own do we give thee.'

15

THE BATTLE WON

God, in His mercy, has far from forgotten me. Still, I wait for my healing; still, I harbour a private prayer that He will one day see fit to restore my sight. But the anxiety has gone from that prayer altogether.

I used to offer up to Him all sorts of good reasons for dealing with me in this way. Giving God reasons for adopting my plans instead of, or in spite of, His own ideas—because of circumstances that He might not have thought of—seems an odd thing to do, but we all do it! This style of prayer brings a smile to the lips, as we recall schoolboy prayers, such as, 'Lord, if the headmaster doesn't punish me too painfully, I will go to church every Sunday, from now on!' or, 'Give me what I need to pass this exam, and I'll be a Christian for ever!' He answers such prayers in His own ways. I did, at one point, suggest that restored vision would be very much in God's interest, as it would enable me to read, meditate on, and generally study the Bible, and therefore be a better servant as a result. His answer came, not as I had dreamed of, but in the shape of a computer, capable of reading text out loud. This feature, coupled with four versions of the Bible and a wordprocessor at fingertip control, actually allows easier, deeper and faster access than many sighted people have! God has His own way of answering.

The next most important frustration, which I offered as

a justification for restoration to full vision, was my lack of independence. Wanting to be able to move around, and visit; to teach away from home; to go easily and regularly to church, and to visit friends, presents enormous drawbacks, when one is having to rely constantly on the goodwill of others to offer lifts. I managed to find an easy way to swallow this guilt, by kidding myself that I was merely asking others to share in the spreading of the healing gospel. It sounds pretty dramatic, and very holy—but this excuse never stood up, when what I really needed to do was go down to the shopping centre and choose a birthday card, or find my way to the post office! In the end, always having to have someone else there, to find a chair for me, or to stop me from bumping into the end of a queue, was building up a guilty conscience—to the point at which it became a lot easier just not to go to this meeting, or that church, at all.

God's answer was in the provision of a guide dog, called Yates. This great and noble black Labrador is a constant companion and faithful friend. He is an ongoing reminder that God's undying love and forgiveness is quite unconditional. Not just a bringer of great joy, he is becoming a necessary part of the ministry at the Well, by adoring broken children, and providing someone to cuddle, just at the right moment, in times of prayer with damaged people. Many months of highly skilled training is given to these animals, at considerable expense, and the results are only to be marvelled at. And yet, one thing seemed missing at the end of my own training time at the Guide Dog Centre. Yates knew about cars and pavement edges, avoiding lamp posts, and finding his way around every conceivable obstacle that might come our way. He knew all the right tricks: how to avoid old ladies who are walking backwards out of shop doorways, as they discuss their various medical operations; and how to use the 'wet nose in the back of the knees' technique to clear a path through chatting shoppers and church congregations. He knew how to behave perfectly in public, and how to get to the Well and back home again. But had he been taught about Jesus? The day we came home from training together, I sat on the garden seat, and told him: "Now that you've come home, we must get down to some serious discussion about the Lord!" His reaction was to flee, straight down the garden, only to dive headlong into the fishpond. We have never looked back!

Of course, I still have to ask for help from the driving members of the Well Centre, when asked to go up country to preach in rural churches, and that sort of trip; but the daily round to work and back is now just him and me. His behaviour is absolutely impeccable—well, most of the time. Within a few months of his arrival, we were asked to address a clergy conference in a hotel, one Saturday. Yates lay, for nearly two hours, on the speakers' platform, fast asleep at my feet, while I waited my turn to speak, and then gave my all to the listening crowd. No-one would have known he was there. Lunchtime saw us following the delegates to the back of the hall and into the hotel restaurant, where he scootled under the table, and went back to sleep through the meal time, precisely according to the training manual; and no bother to anyone. We followed the delegates back into the conference room, and began to walk sedately through them, towards the platform, for the afternoon session. Something felt wrong. All was not well with the strange way he was walking, and with the way he held his head. Exploring my hand down his neck and over his face, I came across an enormous bread bun, clasped firmly in his teeth, and held high and proud, like the spoils of battle. A distinct sense of victory hung in the air! Where did that prize come from? Half dying of shame, in front of all those church leaders, I yanked away most of the offending object, while Yates swallowed the rest with a gulp which seemed to set up a booming echo around the silent and expectant room. Everyone must have heard it!

I was now still approaching the platform, and about to turn and face the audience, with a dog in one hand and a great soggy mass of horridness in the other. What to do with it? As gracefully as possible, I asked an older gentleman on the front row if he would hold on to something for just a moment, and I left it with him. What he did with it, I shall never know, but I would love to have his thoughts framed on the wall above my desk!

A further, huge disadvantage of poor sight is that study, other than the biblical kind, is practically impossible. So I kept down in my depths those feelings, from all those years before, that I should become a clergyman. Now that my sight has almost entirely gone, there would be no way to study theology or church history, or whatever would be required of an applicant. The Well Centre was really on its feet by now, but it lacked a degree of the Church's authority which I, for one, could sense was missing. Spending one's life in a ministry which must be so open to the Holy Spirit also brings with it the need to demonstrate that authority, and to be seen to be under it. A clergyman in charge would be the right answer. Without any method of study, I was reluctant to re-offer myself for training for ordination, for fear of rejection again, on the grounds of impracticality. "Lord," I prayed, "if I could see enough to read, I would apply again. I'll take the risk of all that hurt of rejection again, if it is what you want."

The trustees of the Well even began serious discussions on the need to advertise, to find such a person to lead our efforts. God had the answer to that one, too. A number of conversations with the bishop led, to my astonishment, to an invitation from him. Unprompted by me, this bolt came straight out of the blue: "Would you like me to ordain you?"

The day that 'battlefield commission' became a reality was the day I finally stopped praying for new eyes. Since the earlier rejection for ordination training, I had been taught to forgive and to accept. Now, I was called to holy orders; not, this time, through any personal urging, but just allowing God to work His will. Truly, with such blessings given, I was at last at peace in the arms of God. This prayer of heartfelt thanks lies on the surface of everyday life:

You prepare a table before me in the presence of my enemies, You anoint my head with oil; My cup runs over. Surely goodness and mercy shall follow me all the days of my life; And I will dwell in the house of the LORD forever. Amen.

Psalm 23:6

So, to the question, 'What is a blind man doing running a Christian healing centre?' the real answer is that only God really knows, for it is part of His plan and purpose. This much I have learned, along the struggling road to find peace: God is God. He is the one with majesty and power and glory. He is the creator, the giver of life and, for those who offer, He is the one who bends His plan for the world, to include the new resource just presented to Him. Prayer requests for our personal needs are always heard, and always answered; the latter fact being right at the heart of so much doubt. It is easy to accept there being the two types of answer: 'yes' and 'yes, but not just now'. So much seemingly unanswered prayer is justified by Christians, as being alright, under the heading 'God's timing is perfect'. In truth, the Almighty God has a third answer, too: 'no'. God has never lowered Himself to explain or excuse this answer to me; He is the great God of heaven and earth, and all I can do is accept it as being the right thing as far as He is concerned. I confess that I do not always like it, because it does not seem 'good' to me, but then I am frequently reminded of the question: 'Since when did mankind really know what was good?' Certainly, Adam and Eve thought they knew best, and just look what happened as a result.

Whatever God's answer is, I can only accept it, say, 'thank you' very tentatively, and offer back whatever is received, or not, with an open palm. Offering, thanksgiving, transformation; and receiving anew, only to give again, is the key to this peace in adversity. For me, to allow my disability to govern my existence would be a sin, because it dissociates me from the victory of the Cross. Never did I see this more clearly than on the guide dog training course. Here I was, locked away for four weeks with nine other blind people, and well in position to observe what damage is done, when disability lies at the hub of life, instead of Jesus Christ.

There were some there who had recently become blind, and some had been this way all their lives; but a common thread ran through the group: their resentment, anger and bitterness lay across their hearts, to one degree or another. Such negative reactions are often toxic to the personality.

Worse still, this poison soon began to infect me, too. How depressing it is to others to hear of nothing else but sadness, loneliness, unhappiness and frustration. The absence of light leaves a great darkness. To have Jesus Christ at the centre of my view of life alters all that, and conveys a message into the heavenlies, which blesses me when I think of it. Ephesians 3:10 says that His intent is that now, through the Church, the manifold wisdom of God should be made known to the rulers and authorities in the heavenly realms, according to His eternal purpose, which He accomplished in Christ Jesus our Lord.

Satan is not concerned about our illnesses or tragedies; he just loves to see our faith dwindle, through the suffering which accompanies them. Our battles are not primarily against suffering, but against our own reactions to it. True healing and wholeness is not always found in the cleansing of disease. The projection of the light of Jesus' love, even in times of suffering and illness, is the greater witness. Our lows, our depression times, our frustration and our anger; our weary faith and, at worst, our dismissal of the idea of a good God—these are Satan's little victories in the world. These are the easy things to give in to, and these are the most important battles of all.

Why should the Christian not suffer? It is through our pains that God builds a two lane highway right through the middle of our hearts, so that He can reach other people through us: and that others may reach the Father through Jesus. When this life ends, and I fly up to the bosom of my Father, I would like to think I can look back down, and overhear Satan turn to his generals, saying, "Well, well, there's a thing! After all we could throw at him, he still claims that Jesus Christ is the Lord and Saviour of his life!"

This extract from a group of my poems goes a long way to express my innermost thoughts and feelings on life, and may serve others whose faith has been so tested in the fires of life:

I will praise the Lord all the days of my life;
As long as I live, I will lift His holy Name on high.
I see the years rolled out ahead of me,
They lead ever deeper into His open arms.
The way before me is the Lord's;
His Son is shepherd to my soul along the highway.
To the left and to the right are many pot holes;
I wander from side to side, stumbling and falling
but always going on.

The whiteness of your cloak is a beacon in the darkness;
Your rod and your staff keep me along your ways.
Why, Lord, do I doubt your helping hand?
Why do I dread losing sight of you?
You have promised to guide me through the fiery pits;
You have sworn never to leave me in the dark places.
You are the Lord who shuts the mouths of the lions,
You are the God who protects me from the thorns and briars.
You shield me from those who delight in bringing pain
And from those whose mouths are sweet and whose
hearts are evil.

All my days I will love your name;
All my life I will search to obey your commands.
Your grace and mercy flow over me; my salvation
surrounds me with safety.
You are the Lord, my Saviour; in you I will put all my trust.

I am greatly encouraged in my discipleship by the thought that Jesus, too, must have felt rejected in this world; as I have done, over large chunks of life so far—though for hugely differing reasons, of course. The fellow-feeling, the part-understanding of how he must have felt, lingers on; but, nowadays, this feeling of closeness is not so much one of sharing rejection, for that rejection is all but healed, but of a natural closeness to the one whose body was broken for the life of the world. My eyes have been directly used by God, in His grace, as a positive force, pushing me out of the world in which I craved success, into His world of love, healing and wholeness. The road of love and healing is the one Jesus chose, in obedience to the Father's will, and it is the one along which I have to follow as his disciple, cross on shoulder, on the way set for me.

Yet another point about suffering, which I would never even have guessed at thirty years ago, on the river bank, is that it is sometimes in suffering that we begin to trust God. At first sight, I would have imagined the opposite to be true! If I had been asking, 'If there is a good God, then how is this happening to me?' then the easy conclusion would be to doubt God's existence altogether. However, the more sight I have lost over the years, the more I have found a tremendous need to trust God, for just about everything; and, as one would expect, the more trust one has in another person, the closer those two parties come together.

The more I have travelled into blindness, the more chance there is of things going wrong. I am less and less dependent on my own skills to keep things on the straight and narrow. I have learned to trust God to take care of me, and the people and things I care about. I am beginning to learn something about obedience.

We considered earlier the story of Job. At its beginning, we see a saga unfold, of which Job is completely unaware. God and Satan discuss him, behind his back and out of his earshot. God declares that Job is a good and righteous man, who trusts Him. Satan's response to God, about the level of Job's trust, has certainly been just as relevant to me, in years gone by. Satan suggests to God that it is a relatively easy thing to trust in Him when all is going well, and that, if health and financial security were to be taken away from Job, it would be possible to see just how strong his faith and trust really turn out to be. So, for reasons that I can only say are part of the mystery of God, He allowed Satan to have his way. Job's relationship with God was at stake, and more than severely tested, but by the end of that book a whole new—and deeper—relationship between Job and God has blossomed out of his suffering.

God has never once seen fit to stoop down and explain Himself to me, nor to give me physical healing, but He is gracious enough to keep on repeating the same words: "Trust me; just trust me".

In the end, we can only leave situations of trouble and pain in God's hands. We may not like it; we may not understand it—but God either holds the whole world in His hands, or He does not. It seems to have taken so many years of searching, only to find that there is no middle ground to stand on. Either I trust Him or I deny Him. Psalm 46 encourages me in my conclusion that we have nothing to fear, 'Though the earth give way and the mountains fall into the heart of the sea, though its waters roar and foam and the mountains quake with their surging....' Later in that psalm, God says: "Be still, and know that I am God." If there is a message for me, in the trials and sorrows— through all the little griefs and depressions, as well as the big ones—then surely this is going to be it. The God and Father of our Lord Jesus Christ is sovereign. Suffering is not, in itself, a 'good'—for suffering, pain, sickness and disease stem from the disobedience of mankind, beginning with the Fall. The Bible makes it clear that God wants a perfect, loving relationship with us. We are enabled to enjoy such a restored relationship, because of the grace of God, through faith in Jesus, who died on the Cross of Calvary, that we might live.

Accepting the cup the Father offers us may involve suffering— Jesus warns his disciples of this—but such suffering is not meaningless, for we are promised that, 'All things work together for good, for those who love God.'

I wanted from God either my healing, or a decent explanation as to why He would not give it to me. What I have been given is a growing sense of the purpose of my 'cup', as I learnt to offer everything back to Him, thanking Him that He has a loving plan and purpose for me—even if my cup had to include suffering. We praise God for the healing we see at the Well; but, in my experience, as we begin to thank Him, and to offer ourselves (especially our feelings) back to

Him, what He then gives is always good—whether it includes physical healing or not. In great compassion, Jesus comes to all who come to him, and that is the best gift of all.

Made in the USA
Charleston, SC
13 May 2012